"In guiding us in our pursuit of the abundant life, Wayne rightly encourages us to understand 'it is found within the imperfect particulars of our lives.'"

—BILL THRALL, leadership mentor; coauthor, *TrueFaced*

"Spiritually perceptive and refreshing, this book is truly a gift to our get-it-done, performance-oriented Christian culture. I love Wayne's unique and personal style, humorous touches, and real courage as he confronts head-on the realities of personal faith."

—BOB MITCHELL, past president, Young Life

"In this wonderful book, Wayne Brown shows us how grace works. It is not an achievement to be earned but a mystery to be received."

—M. CRAIG BARNES, author, *When God Interrupts*

WATER *from* STONE

WHEN "RIGHT CHRISTIAN LIVING" HAS LEFT YOU SPIRITUALLY DRY

M. WAYNE BROWN

NAVPRESS®
BRINGING TRUTH TO LIFE

The Navigators is an international Christian organization. Our mission is to reach, disciple, and equip people to know Christ and to make Him known through successive generations. We envision multitudes of diverse people in the United States and every other nation who have a passionate love for Christ, live a lifestyle of sharing Christ's love, and multiply spiritual laborers among those without Christ.

NavPress is the publishing ministry of The Navigators. NavPress publications help believers learn biblical truth and apply what they learn to their lives and ministries. Our mission is to stimulate spiritual formation among our readers.

© 2004 by Marvin Wayne Brown

NAVPRESS, BRINGING TRUTH TO LIFE, and the NAVPRESS logo are registered trademarks of NavPress. Absence of ® in connection with marks of NavPress or other parties does not indicate an absence of registration of those marks.

ISBN 1-57683-471-9

Cover design by Brand Navigation, LLC (The Office of Bill Chiaravalle)
www.brandnavigation.com
Cover photo: Steve Gardner, His Image Pixel Works
Creative Team: Don Simpson, Amy Spencer, Darla Hightower, Pat Miller

Some of the anecdotal illustrations in this book are true to life and are included with the permission of the persons involved. All other illustrations are composites of real situations, and any resemblance to people living or dead is coincidental.

Unless otherwise identified, all Scripture quotations in this publication are taken from the HOLY BIBLE: NEW INTERNATIONAL VERSION® (NIV®). Copyright © 1973, 1978, 1984 by International Bible Society. Used by permission of Zondervan Publishing House. All rights reserved. Other versions used include: the *New King James Version* (NKJV). Copyright © 1982 by Thomas Nelson, Inc. Used by permission. All rights reserved.

Brown, M. Wayne.
  Water from stone : when "right Christian living" has left you spiritually dry / M. Wayne Brown.
     p. cm.
Includes bibliographical references.
  ISBN 1-57683-471-9
  1. Spiritual life. 2. Spiritual formation. I. Title.
  BV4501.3.B77 2004
  248.4--dc22
                                        2003023817

Printed in Canada

1 2 3 4 5 6 7 8 9 10 / 08 07 06 05 04

FOR A FREE CATALOG OF NAVPRESS BOOKS & BIBLE STUDIES,
CALL 1-800-366-7788 (USA) OR 1-416-499-4615 (CANADA)

For Beth,

my wild rose

Except in idea, perfection is as wild
as light; there is no hand laid on it.
But the house is a shambles unless
the vision of its perfection
upholds it like stone.

WENDELL BERRY, "THE DESIGN OF A HOUSE"

CONTENTS

ACKNOWLEDGMENTS

*R*ecalling the legion of people who have contributed to this book is a little like seeing a curtain call at the end of a rousing musical. Before you know it, the stage is filled to capacity and you wonder where all of these people came from and how it is that you are so fortunate to have crossed paths with each one.

Of this cast of characters, I am most singularly grateful to Don Simpson, my remarkably talented and attentive editor at NavPress, who set this whole thing in motion. Don, thank you for pursuing me, for giving me your time and encouragement, and—most importantly—for giving me the gift of your friendship.

I want to thank Dan Rich and Terry Behimer, also at NavPress, for their enthusiasm and willingness to embrace a project of this nature. My thanks go as well to Amy Spencer for her careful work behind the scenes.

To Jody Rein, my agent for this book and the one before it, I will always be grateful. In holding me to what often seemed to be impossible standards, you helped get me from thought to print.

My mother, brother, and sister—unflagging in their support and love—have always been an inspiration. And, Dad, thank you for loving me from beyond the grave by showing up in my dreams and memories at just the right times.

I didn't realize until I was well along in the writing of this book just how influential my grandfather had been in helping me engage the complexities and sit with the mysteries of life's joys and sorrows. Grandpa Allen, what a tidal force you were in my life.

From my brave, forthright clients I am constantly gleaning the real-life stuff that lends its authenticity to a book such as this. I thank each one of you for letting me in beyond the surface. When I think back over the past twenty-some years, it is your willingness to openly consider the often-difficult truths in your lives that has inspired me to consider my own.

The scrappy, stimulating, and always unorthodox "regulars" at The Market, Sweet Rockin' Coffee, and Tattered Cover Book Store kept me thinking outside the box. Thank you all for accepting me into your lives and, in some cases, into your homes.

And finally, at center stage, my wife, Beth, and my daughter, Paige: Beth, you are nothing less than a phenomenon.

How you manage to be a great mom and wife, stay beautiful and witty, help keep a house running and, then, to bang
the gavel in your courtroom everyday, is beyond my com-
prehension. You and I know how pivotal you have been in
making the emotional and practical sacrifices necessary to
keep a writer writing. You have given above and beyond the
call and I will always love you for it. And, Paige, you are the
most wonderful creature God ever made. What a joy you are
in my life.

INVITATION TO A JOURNEY

---~⁓~---

*F*orever etched in my memory is a scene that unfolded several winters ago on one of the back roads that wind through the Amish farmlands of Pennsylvania. I had just concluded a speaking engagement in nearby Mount Holly, New Jersey, and was enjoying a casual tour of the surrounding area from the passenger seat of my host's sedan, when a horse and black carriage appeared over a distant hill. Viewed through a surreal soup of fog and light snow, the road seemed to ebb and swell— all but tossing the primitive buggy and its occupants into the adjoining field.

Then, as if rising out of the ground behind it, an eighteen wheeler—spitting ice and spraying steam and slush from its wheels and iron nostrils—came bearing down on the tiny transport like a frothing bull.

From my front-seat vantage point, it looked as though the clip-cloppers were doomed. But the truck's driver ably threaded his rig between buggy and broken centerline without incident, and my heart began beating once again. "We see that all the time on these roads," said my host.

"Really?" I responded. "I never knew what I was missing."

In an alarming way, a similar scene is unfolding today on the seemingly peaceful, pastoral road traveled by the people of God—a contest so close to most of us that we are unaware it's happening. This scene involves a sort of duel between an eighteen wheeler Christianity and a quieter but more essential faith.

Rising on the horizon of the church's pilgrim way is a pragmatic and programmatic approach to faith that is so convincing, so pervasive, so widely accepted, that we are often impotent to resist its influence. For lack of a better term, I identify this force as the culture of Right Christian Living. In one form or another, this force usually shows up as a set of "biblical principles," assembled to achieve what is often a noble objective: perhaps a stronger marriage, better-behaved kids, more effective prayer, a larger church, even political influence. But invariably another set of subtle, unstated messages attend these themes: that more and more control of my life will be delivered into my hands through these principles; that God essentially guarantees to bless this effort; and that these attention-getting programs somehow contain the primary purposes of God and of the Christian life. If you do these things, they advertise, you'll get the

results you're looking for. The promises are so compelling
and the promotion so exciting that we feel obliged to pro-
claim, "This most certainly is God's way!"

Let me hasten to acknowledge that I believe God can
and does use such programs. But what I'm concerned about
is that something important can be lost—and, I maintain,
often *is* lost—along the way. What I hope to expose in this
book is a mindset that to some degree we have subtly
absorbed from our technological culture and superimposed
onto our Christian faith. Its iron will of efficiency is mecha-
nizing our relationships with God and other people and
squeezing the very life out of our freedom, love, and joy. A
few years ago, Eugene H. Peterson playfully—but also
prophetically, and even sternly—wrote a letter from Jesus
Christ "To the Suburban Church of North America." I believe
Peterson's words would benefit the whole church as well. A
portion of his letter reads:

> But I have this against you: you're far too
> impressed with Size and Power and Influence. You
> are impatient with the small and the slow. You
> exercise little discernment between the ways of the
> world and my ways. It distresses me that you so
> uncritically copy the attitudes and methods that
> make your life in suburbia work so well. You grab

onto anything that works and looks good. You do so
many good things, but too often you do them in the
world's way instead of mine, and so you seriously
compromise your obedience.[1]

I believe the challenge for the church in the twenty-first
century is to return to our first love—not only to the *Person*
of our first love, but also to the *way* of our first love—the
way of Jesus Christ. This pursuit will require us to uncover
what is wrong with some of today's dominant approaches
to spiritual life, and to seek instead Christ's truer way.

In essence, I hope to help us recover our ability to see
with eyes of faith. This will necessitate use of our imaginative powers, for we must break through the mechanistic
confinements of Right Christian Living into what I call
"love's freedom." This is the place to which I believe God
repeatedly tried to bring the Israelites—beginning with the
Exodus—a place God called "a good and spacious land."[2]
It was a place free of the confining slavery imposed by the
surrounding culture, Pharaoh's Egypt.

Our slavery today only appears to be different. Sure, we
pride ourselves on our Western political freedoms. But
underneath—as with the people of God in Egypt—we are
oppressed in ways we're not fully aware of by the numbing
reductionism of our technological culture.

God's goal is the same for us: to bring us out into a good and spacious land where we may enjoy a mutually loving relationship with him. This is the place of love's freedom. As King David said, "He brought me out into a spacious place; he rescued me because he delighted in me."[3] God's delight is love's freedom. And the experience of God's delight is our deepest, most meaningful delight as well.

But there is a paradox. I will argue that the place of love's freedom is not a distant land, not a place of escape, but an inner sanctuary shaped by our existing commitments, relationships, anguishes, and longings. It is a place that sometimes feels like impossible confinement. But, this is the place inhabited by One who experienced the ultimate confinement as God on a cross. In this book, I hope to show you that he will set you free in the least obvious place—right where you are.

In my two decades of counseling followers of Christ, I have seen the damage created by our temptation to latch onto patterns of faith that expect certain results from God and are deeply discouraged when things don't turn out as promised. The culture of Right Christian Living is a set of assumptions that can serve to cover up deeper issues in our relationships, our sexuality, our work life, our thought life, our emotional life, our questioning ache for the real presence of the living God—issues that are crying out for the gospel's transformation. These are things that aren't quickly changed by practical steps and principles, but require a deeper, more meditative gaze into the mirror of God's Word.

The essential truth that God is intimately with us—in our sometimes unbearable commitments, in the loneliness and anguish of our broken hearts and failing bodies, in the joy and wonder of life's most simple gifts—is being trampled by our feverish attempts to form a faith that "works," a faith that becomes more an effort to conjure or seduce God than to engage in waiting, seeking, passionate relationship with him.

In promising that a such-and-such approach to parenting will yield an exceptional child or that praying a certain ancient prayer will attract God's blessings, this kind of Christianity woos us away from the very One it proclaims. For sure, we've become sophisticated in our detection of a "works mentality." We've learned to scale back some of our busyness and breathe the freeing air of God's grace. But things still have to get done. Our bodies and our lives and our families still have needs— often great and desperate needs.

And so grace becomes more a word than a power received, more a doctrine than a living practice, and we fall back into the same old pattern of looking for effective means to solve our problems. Life becomes stale again. Instead of breathing the liberating air of grace, we're suffo- cating in the impersonal smog of our pragmatism.

Sociologist Anthony Giddens writes: "Trust in abstract systems provides for the security of day-to-day reliability, but by its very nature cannot supply either the mutuality or intimacy which personal trust relations offer."[4]

One of our goals in this book will be to discover what is blocking our "personal trust relations" with God and other people. We cannot entirely blame our technological culture for our situation. Our problem is an ancient one, with roots deep in the history of human nature—indeed, deep in the history of God's people. In Psalm 78 we see how the Israelites' attempt to force God's hand was not the way of a personal trust relation. The psalmist tells us, "They spoke against God, saying, '. . . When he struck the rock, water gushed out, and streams flowed abundantly. But can he also give us food? Can he supply meat for his people?'"[5]

They missed the point, just as we so often do. In their impatience to get what they felt they not only lacked, but were entitled to, the Israelites came to prefer the tangibility of God's visible miracles over the dependability of his unseen but eternal character.

Today's Right Christian Living approach tries to force what could be but isn't quite yet—the perfect Christian life, peace and harmony, effective ministry, the Promised Land. The second orientation (what I will call in this book "transformation-based faith") waits and watches in faith to see what already is but is not readily seen.

Transformation-based faith imagines God with us moment by moment, regardless of how things might seem. Although in the gospel of Christ we encounter elements of each approach, we are more often throwing our collective, tragically imbalanced weight behind the first: Right Christian Living. We assuage our discomfort with the mystery of God's ways and our impatience for satisfying results by *doing* the Christian life instead of *being* one of Christ's. We need both, of course. Philosopher William Barrett writes, "The truth of human life must perpetually lie in the tension between being and doing."[6] Even more, in this book we will aim to acquire a new discernment for pursuing present-mindedness in the midst of our working, for waiting on God in the midst of all our action.

In these pages I seek to immerse us in a transformation-based faith. A faith where the fantastic—though sometimes difficult to see—is anything but fantasy. Here I will ask you to imagine a God whose presence is so accessible, so immediate, that it requires no grand entrance, no special song and dance, no proof of purchase beyond the cross of Christ. I will ask you to imagine a God whose powers and purposes are so far beyond even the fantastic that we are relieved and grateful he did not bend to what we demanded.

Faith in *this* God does not require as its validation per-fect kids, a burgeoning church, or miraculous answers to our desperate prayers for relief from life's troubles. The mir-acles that the God of *this* faith performs (although he can and does perform the other sort as well) are more typically realized in the gritty engagements of daily life or in the still-ness of the night resounding deep within one's soul. However, this transformation-based faith will also have the effect of shifting the longings of our hearts, and in some way redeeming even the pain that prompts our anxious prayers for relief.

As you turn these pages, I hope to surprise you with a God who inhabits the nooks and crannies of your present life—indeed, the cracks and hollows of the very stones you tread every day—a God who will at once taunt, perplex, satisfy, challenge, disappoint, touch, teach, jolt, and exhila-rate you. For I believe that, with a subtle but transforming shift in perspective, the apparently mundane tasks and com-mitments in your life—yes, even your hardships and heartaches—are stones from which the deepest healing and nourishment of the Savior can flow.

Is this really possible?

Well, for the moment, at least, just imagine . . .

Part One

THE
IMAGINATIVE
SPIRIT

chapter 1

Imagining a Truer Way

The man who cannot quietly close his eyes,
certain that there is vision after vision
inside, simply waiting until nighttime
to rise all around him in the darkness —
it's all over for him, he's like an old man.
RAINER MARIA RILKE, *The Book of Hours*

I muscled the sleeping bag strap on my Holubar frame pack another inch into its buckle and turned to help my friend, Greg, with his. It was a morning in the summer of '78, and we had awakened exhausted. Though ultimately successful, our previous day's quest to conquer Colorado's Mount Holy Cross had nearly cost us our lives.

The climb to the summit had gone well. As was typical of these "fourteener" adventures, the morning weather was crisp and clear, the view from the top, grand and glorious.[1] However, by early afternoon—again, par for these mountains—dark, aggressive clouds had gathered like a herd of snorting rhinoceros to stampede in our direction. Weighing in somewhere between novice and capable, we made the worse-than-novice mistake of thinking we could beat the storm down the mountain. Worse still, we decided to take the most direct route.

Soon we found ourselves inching our way like suction-toed tree frogs down the slick, icy cliffs of this shale crevice "shortcut." For nearly three hours we dug our boots and fingers into the unforgiving walls of our precarious nightmare. At long last, as the storm passed and the remaining light returned, we were able to extract our frozen bodies from the mountain's angular face, finish the descent, and indulge in a fitful night's sleep back at camp.

"Let's just put one foot in front of the other," Greg said the following morning, "and go home." As I mumbled something in response, a man carrying waders and a fishing pole stepped off the main trail and walked toward us.

"You boys havin' a good time?" he asked. Greg and I looked at each other and laughed.

"Yeah—a real good time."

"Headed back to Half Moon trailhead?" he inquired.

Our packs already felt harsh and heavy on our aching shoulders as we steeled our resolve to reach the valley's base, climb back up and over the next ridge, and then finish the final, short descent to Half Moon with as little effort as possible.

"Yes, headed back," I said flatly. Apparently, not getting the message that we would rather be walking than talking, the fisherman leaned toward us like a street thief about to show us his trench-coat cache of wristwatches and whispered, "I know another way."

I saw Greg's wry smile. We were thinking the same thing: another shortcut—no thanks.

"Not many people know about it," he continued. "I'm not sure it's a time-saver, necessarily, but it's a lot more adventurous."

I took the bait. "So how far down the trail is it?" I asked, skepticism now oozing from my voice.

"Oh, it's right behind you," he said.

Turning, I found myself staring at a talus slope—a steep ridge of displaced earth and stone created by the bulldozing nose of some ancient glacier. "I see nothing but a pile of rocks," I said, my irritation mounting.

"You see, that's the beauty of it," he continued. "You can't see it unless you know what you're lookin' for."

"Why on earth would we want to climb all the way up those rocks to find a trail we can't see that won't get us any more quickly to the place we're going?" I huffed.

"That depends on if you want to just get back, or if you want to get back satisfied," he replied, a hint of mischief in his leathery voice. "Now, you boys have a nice day."

There are those defining moments in life when something invades the rational cells in your brain and you find yourself helplessly heeding some alien force. This was such a moment.

Like spring athletes running stadium stairs, we instantly found ourselves clawing and churning our way up the side of the ridge.

About a minute and thirty feet into the climb, we collapsed onto the flat surface of a three-foot-wide ledge. This ledge, the by-product of the junction between our talus slope and the cliff behind it, had formed a small incision-like path that ran south along the cliff's face toward several small outcroppings of oak brush and pine. A quarter of a mile beyond that, the trail disappeared into denser vegetation.

Greg and I gave each other a thumbs-up, steadied our packs, and headed off toward Half Moon. Within minutes I felt a fresh surge of energy. Like one of Snow White's insufferable dwarves, I started humming "heigh-ho" and was about to burst into full-throated song when I remembered that Greg was right behind me. Grateful that I hadn't yet started skipping like Sneezy or Doc, I self-consciously cleared my throat and resumed my manly man stride.

Granite footing soon yielded to a more forgiving forest floor. Light streaming through a mottled canopy of branches and leaves cast a puzzle of shadows across our path. A euphoric feeling that I had just entered Lewis's Narnia or—who knew—perhaps even Tolkien's Mordor, overpowered my apprehension. Greg and I paused. This was an enchanted place. I felt strangely at peace and refreshingly alive. Forming in my consciousness was a vague but tingling feeling that God was up to something—what, exactly, I did not know. Having initially taken this mountain for granted, I had been both humbled and revived by its astonishing character.

Stirred by my encounter with Mount Holy Cross, the following year became a year of questions, an unexpected journey into the heart of my deeper spiritual motives and intentions. Had I taken my faith—my God—for granted as well? Had I become so enamored with the promise of faith's benefits that I could not appreciate its textures, its mysteries? Would I continue to pound the rutted path of faith-as-usual, or would I heed *another* fisherman's voice?

And so began a journey that has yet to let me go.

THE THREE CHRISTIAN CULTURES:
INDUSTRIOUSNESS, NUMBNESS, AND PASSION

For all our modern spiritual frenzy, we Christians are mostly a people without passion or imagination. We shuffle up and down the trail of our initial conversion . . . up and down . . .

up and down . . . beating the same path to the foot of the mountain of Christian assumptions, pushing the same limbs from our faces, pointing out to our similarly engaged companions the same spiritual mile markers.

To be sure, we are driven, active, at times even consumed with our Christian endeavors. But rarely are we passionate. Rarely are our wills fully given to personal transformation into the *way* Christ thought, spoke, and acted. Instead we too quickly seek restoration over transformation, blessing over brokenness, a standard Christian life over a vital faith open to God's unpredictable adventure. We seek instead a safe and well-trodden path to faith's high mountains, and feel confused—if not betrayed—when storms and shadows appear.

Out of the tangled collision between what we long ago expected of faith and what we actually awaken to each morning, three general responses always seem to emerge: industriousness, numbness, or passion. Although there is a great deal of overlap in these orientations to faith, for the purpose of contrast I ask you to indulge me in this initial, overstated depiction of each type.

Industriousness

The industrious Christian's formula reads something like this: combine the perfect understanding of God with the perfect obedience and you have the perfect Christian who is perfectly pleasing to God. "Be perfect, therefore, as your heavenly Father is perfect," she fondly quotes from Matthew 5:48. Again, this is an overstatement to make a point. But somewhere inside us there's the sense that, "If I do this, I will get that." We grew up steeped in this instrumental reasoning—from parents, teachers, employers, our culture. We apply it to our spiritual lives as well. We're glad to find a handful of practical steps to achieve maturity in each of a dozen areas. It keeps things simple. We can then "master" the Christian life. Of course, as followers of Christ, we know we fail—and then we fall on our faces in humility before God and ask his forgiveness. We claim Christ's righteousness. But, then—with nothing to fill the void of our inaction—we go back to doing, to trying a little harder. We forget, as French lay theologian Jacques Ellul reminds us, that: "The whole frenzied effort of well-intentioned man has been crushed. At a stroke we learn that in Jesus Christ salvation is given to us, that God loved us before we did anything, that all is grace; grace—gracious gift, free gift."[2]

Numbness

The numb Christian's initial approach is identical to the industrious one's. At some point, however, the numb one can no longer suppress a nagging, visceral awareness that this approach (though very busy on the surface) leapfrogs over a basic truth: one cannot secure the bridge to God any more perfectly or impressively than Christ already has. The numb Christian is numb, not because he doesn't know what to do, but because he has *done* and *done* until he feels completely undone. Believing that he must either get on board with the industrious perfecting of his faith or resign himself to the fact that he just doesn't have what it takes to dance the industrious dance, he becomes either disheartened or cynical. Hanging his weary head, or perhaps steeling his cynical jaw, he goes through the agonizing motions of faith. With faith's imaginative nerve effectively severed, he lives a half-throttle life.

Passion

The passionate Christian sees things a little differently. While acknowledging the indispensable importance of becoming theologically equipped and pursuing the best for God's kingdom, the passionate Christian understands that without the heart's impassioned response to the bare-bones love *of* God and *for* God, her efforts are no more than noisy brass and clanging cymbals.

The passionate one enjoys the unfolding of the story as much as knowing how it will end. She understands that becoming attuned to and falling in love with the Author himself—his cadence, his genius at weaving the disparate parts of the story into a breathtaking whole, his exquisite fondness for his creatures—is really the point of the adventure, after all.

The passionate one is far more interested in God's presence than his presents.

Consequently, the passionate person's worship is free of manipulative or obligatory overtones. His prayers are more often requests for wisdom and expressions of gratitude than pleas for some desired outcome. He is aware of the mysterious and sometimes disturbing nature of blessings, and he craves the spiritual eyes with which to see their surprises and complexities.

All said, the truly passionate person is fully alive—here, now. She greets each day with the abundant, unedited joy, pain, and intrigue of her existence.

In contrast, both industrious and numb Christians seem far too distracted with straining to get to a place where they *are not* than with being fully present in the place where they *are,* more concerned with producing *for* and getting *from* God than with laying bare the chambers of their hearts.

Why do I see passion as the truer way to travel? Because passion was the way of Christ in his sojourn here on earth. He was fully aware of eternity in the present moment. His approach to life, to others, to his Father, was one of loving intensity. He reached down to lift up the lame, he opened eyes with his hands and his words, he gathered children into his arms, he wept openly, he bled and died for us. Yet, he often waited. He paused for eternity's fullness. He often made others impatient with his schedule or his whereabouts. As unique as he is, he is our model because he is the pioneer and perfecter of *our* faith. He shows us love's perfect freedom.

Again: Why passion? In the next chapter, we will look closely at the Emmaus Road journey of the two disciples and Jesus. For now, I want to point out the importance of the disciples' passion. Jesus, in what the late James Loder of Princeton Seminary used to call "the divine deference," acted as if he were going to continue on his journey past the disciples' destination of Emmaus. It was the disciples' *passionate insistence* ("But they urged him strongly . . . "[3]) that arrested Jesus and made him turn with them into the inn. I find it a stunning thought that our passion influences God. This seems to be what engages his gracious presence with us in a special way on a daily basis.

How can we cultivate passion? That's what we will explore in the chapters to come. But let me say here that, in a sense, we can't cultivate passion. God gives it to us as we wait on him. We must create room for God in our hearts. "Sabbath," Dallas Willard calls it: "Sabbath is a way of life. . . . It sets us free from bondage to our own efforts. Only in this way can we come to the power and joy of a radiant life in ministry, a blessing to all we touch. And yet Sabbath is almost totally absent from the existence of contemporary Christians and their ministers."[4]

IN SEARCH OF A GOLDEN GOD

Although we seem capable of imagining a God who will bless us if we do his bidding, or even a God who will bring a kind of future, holy justice to life's injustices, we are clearly befuddled at the thought of a God who is, himself, the blessing. We have our focus on the endgame of the abundant life, and so we go about our spiritually industrious endeavors. We enthrone the ideal of the perfect Christian man or woman. We entreat one another to grow our kids "God's way," to vote "God's way," to sterilize our communities and social engagements to a degree that none can doubt our blessing-worthy efforts.

And we grow increasingly disheartened and cynical.

Though rarely aloud, we ask, "How can God not bless us when we have been so good? Why does he not reward us with our deserved spoils?" Like the freed Israelites of Exodus 17, we grumble, "Is God here among us, or not?" And yet, all the while, God *is* with us, leading us through our own sea of menacing soldiers, feeding us meat and bread from heaven, giving us water from stone.

So why can't we see this?

We can't see it because this kind of seeing has nothing to do with achievement or arrival. This kind of imaginative spirit has nothing to do with getting to any particular spiritual place but, rather, with seeing more deeply into what is immediately at hand.

We can't see this *deeper* life because we so crave the fantastic *better* one! And we need look no further than the Exodus account to find the roots of this theme of wrangling from God the better life.

When it became clear to the Israelites that freedom from oppression didn't mean freedom from trials and tribulations, they decided to speed the camels more quickly toward the Promised Land by taking matters into their own hands. Although God seemed to be slow and miserly in his care for them, they weren't going to let him stop them from getting what they wanted. Yes, he had done a pretty good job of extracting them from Pharaoh's bondage. And granted, there was the heavenly quail and—oh, yes—that water-from-rock thing. But he had obviously run out of magic. It was time to help God out. It was time to build something big and shiny. Something they could simultaneously admire and manipulate at will. Something so imposing it would do their faith-work for them. Something irresistibly golden.

A TRUER WAY

The shift from a life intent on this kind of spiritual "cashing in" to a life that is available to God's transformational work begins by wrestling with a couple of pesky questions.

The first question reads something like this: Is it possible that we, in our time, are being swept along in a shallow current of safe and simple five-step answers to the Christian life that is carrying us to the wrong ocean?

As a therapist who counsels daily the friendly fire casualties of what seem to be misdirected faith, it's apparent that today's Christian often becomes addicted to seeking solutions rather than true transformation. This addiction is making us spiritually neurotic and ineffective.

We are called to walk a narrow path—one that requires the exercise of faith and a sense of adventure. But we quickly fall prey to a gospel that rarely gets beyond the brush-clearing exercises of sin detection, pain management, and role definition to Christ's overarching concern: the engaging, here-and-now adventure of the kingdom of God.

Recently, I spoke to a group of about eighty MOPS (Mothers of Preschoolers) moms. Knowing that the host church was located in the heart of a posh mountain community, I was curious as to why these moms wanted me to speak to them about depression. What could a community that God had so richly "blessed" possibly be depressed about?

At the conclusion of my talk, I told the group that I would be available for the remainder of the meeting to speak with anyone who had questions or just wanted to chat. An hour and a half later, after addressing the concerns of a dozen moms awash in tears, frustration, anger, disappointment, shock, and hopelessness, I shuffled to my four wheeler to inhale a plate of tasty pumpkin bread and sugar-dusted brownies, and to reflect on what had just transpired. The common theme—*always* the common theme—was some variation of "If I'm doing everything so right, then why are so many things going so wrong?" "I've been working like an obsessed person to get my child to 'first-time obedience,'" said one mom, "and she's still a pill." "Why is my husband so emotionally removed?" asked another. "We have everything you'd want."

It goes without saying that this theme of disillusionment and frustration is not the exclusive property of the rich. It is the one I most commonly run into in the Christian community at large. "What will it take to get God to truly bless me?" we ask. "Is God here among us, or not?"

"Work the program, plug in the solution, reap the rewards" never works. The reason, I believe, is that it places the focus on the efficacy of our efforts instead of on trust in the sufficiency of God's wisdom. It places us squarely in the role of determining what will and what won't be evidence of God's presence in our lives.

This leads us to the second pesky question: Have we become so enamored with the idea of solving (and thereby eliminating) the challenges of faith and life that we have lost a vision for how we can be transformed through those challenges?

Certainly, one of the appealing aspects of Christian faith is the promise of a life filled with meaning and purpose. The density of our existential pain compels us to find antidotes. It is no surprise, then, that we often equate salvation with relief (as did the Israelites). We seek the hidden code, the missing link that will secure our pain-free existence.

However, personal transformation—not situational relief—is the seed of true faith. What it means to truly live is, well, to *live* in the midst of our pain and joy, not in the anesthetizing expectations of how God will rescue us from the very life he has given us. And yet, how alien it would be to think of committing heart and soul to a faith that does *not* value pain relief, "getting it all figured out," or spiritual "arrival" as its primary objectives.

Caught up in a strange hybrid of fear and impatience toward God, we go through the appeasing motions of our rituals, hoping we will do something right that will win us his favor. Much like Atta, the ant princess in the animated film *A Bug's Life,* our faith is sometimes nothing more than the hope

that God—sampling the appeasing spoils of our spiritual productivity and deeming them acceptable—will "come, eat, and
leave" and then bless our socks off with whatever we want.
After all, we have been spiritually diligent. We deserve it.

But how can intimacy possibly exist in a relationship
where our worthiness is measured (and commensurately
rewarded) by the amount and quality of our output?
Nevertheless, we would much rather be productive than personal. One gives us tangible results. The other threatens to
force us, no doubt uncomfortably, out of ourselves. We grav-
itate toward the productive because it's much easier, much
more within our control. The personal always involves
another person—whether God or human—and that's when
things get messy.

Don't get me wrong. I'm for productivity, for sure, and
our "products" should be the best quality we can make
them—but not because God will otherwise slay us or
because they are our ticket to heaven. Rather we aim to
infuse the world around us with the love and life of God,
because our passion for him compels us to do nothing less.

The temptation to emphasize "productive" over "personal" is not new. It occurs famously in the stark extremes of
1 Corinthians 13:3: "If I give all I possess to the poor and sur-
render my body to the flames, but have not love, I gain nothing." True gain comes only through what is usually less

dramatic, but also fully and warmly personal. True gain is humble, but passionate, love for God and other people.

However, for the industrious Christian, even the application of Scripture can lack the personal. Take, for example, 2 Corinthians 9:6-7: "Remember this: Whoever sows sparingly will also reap sparingly, and whoever sows generously will also reap generously. Each man should give what he has decided in his heart to give, not reluctantly or under compulsion, for God loves a cheerful giver." Our temptation is to grasp the first part of this passage with utilitarian self-interest: If I do this, I will get that. I can even call it a "biblical principle," and expect a blessing—or at least use it to erase God's frown. But this is to miss the deeper issue: the call to a joyful abandon of the heart, not to a work of calculating reason. The heart is where a profound, integrating transformation is needed. With our situation already won for us on the cross, we are set free to offer ourselves in ways that elicit this heart response from God: "God loves a cheerful giver."

ENGAGING FAITH'S IMAGINATIVE SPIRIT

So where does all of this talk about different Christian cultures, the search for a golden god, and a "truer way" lead us?

First, it leads us to consider a different way of approaching our faith that imagines the following:

- that God is with us personally—here and now—regardless of how it might sometimes seem,
- that personal transformation—not spiritual industriousness—is what God most delights in,
- that this transformation most often occurs *within*—not in spite of—the commitments we've already made, however challenging.

Looking through these three windows, we can see more clearly how our bruised lives, strained marriages, disappointments with God, maimed bodies, wounded spirits, dazed minds, and private fears are the contexts—not the controlling themes—of our lives.

Second, I hope this discussion will challenge us to consider that the life of faith is not simply one of going up and down the trail while banging the drums of spiritual industry, but of moving more deeply and adventurously into the unfolding story of our own unique commitments. For it is within these commitments that we encounter God and his transformational intentions.

Like the fisherman Greg and I encountered, my desire in this book is to point you toward a path of faith that truly satisfies. I believe this journey will help you become more patient and forgiving in your relationships, wiser in your judgments, more grateful in your abundance, more far-sighted in your commitments, more merciful in your struggles and failures, and more in love with Christ.

I also believe it will lead you toward a more imaginative, passionate faith. And I'm confident that as you make your way, you will begin to see more clearly God's gracious face in the life you're living right now.

Somewhere in boardrooms, hospital wards, jazz clubs, baseball dugouts, homes, movie theaters, and daycare centers, on cruises, in hovels, in bookstores, and even occasionally—to everyone's great surprise and edification—in the pulpit, are those who feel the scars on the Fisherman's outstretched hands and are willing to forsake the crowded, beaten path for the one they can't yet see.

I believe there is a truer, more adventurous way than the one we are currently following. It is a narrow way through faith's high mountains . . . a way where Christ most assuredly goes before us.

chapter 2

IMAGINING A REFRESHING GOD

He paints as one going over a hill, singing.
ROBERT HENRI, *The Art Spirit*

———————— ～ ————————

I would just as soon show my hand right up front.

I believe it is difficult for one to experience a passionate, imaginative faith unless there is a great, personal post-conversion awakening. I'm talking about a shift of heart and mind—from seeing faith as an exercise in being industriously pleasing to God and, therefore, worthy of getting from God the things we ask, to abandoning ourselves to him because he is God. Stated simply, I am convinced that our faith awakens to its passionate core when we become more interested in who God is *in* us than what his presence in our life will *do* for us.

Knowing God is certainly so much more than knowing how the arrangement works, that is, "If I do such and such

for God, then God will do thus and so for me." To truly
know God is to engage the severe and yet strangely refreshing and wondrous wisdom of his beauty and nature.

GOD'S SEVERE BEAUTY

Several months ago my wife, Beth, and I decided it was time
to give our sturdy but cramped old colonial house the gift
of a new kitchen (which, of course, soon metamorphosed
into a multistoried project more financially and invasively
akin to a triple heart bypass than a house renovation).

After talking with several neighbors about their own
adventures in remodeling, it was clear to us that we should
first find an architect who would help us retain our home's
vintage character. Nosing around various neighborhood
renovation projects, I soon compiled a list of seven local
architects. Of these seven, three kept resurfacing. Several
phone calls and schedule readjustments later, interviews
with our top three candidates were set.

The first interview went smoothly enough. The soft-
spoken architect was familiar with the quirks of older homes
and appreciated the fact that we wanted a "seamless" renovation. After our meeting with him, however, we realized
we weren't any closer to an inspiring vision for the project
than we were before. This architect would undoubtedly

have done a good job, but it was clear to us that it would also have been done without heart.

The second architect was a man who obviously knew where to find the information he needed and was focused on getting it. Barely acknowledging my welcome at the front door, he was quickly off to the "scene of the crime" (as he put it). Our exhausting romp through the kitchen, out into the backyard, back into the living room, up and down stairs—his camera flashing the whole time—left me craving a glass of cold water.

Passing through the dining room on his way back to the front door, he suddenly stopped in front of an old, original oil painting hanging on the room's north wall. "Looks like your movers dropped this one," he quipped, referring to several broken leaf motifs on the old gilded picture frame. I smiled. He slung his camera over his neck and was halfway down the sidewalk before turning to say thanks and that he could get his team on the project right away if we hired him and that he would look forward to working with us and would we please call him when we were ready to move forward.

Two down.

Several days later a casually dressed man with a short goatee, friendly demeanor, and picture-filled portfolio arrived for his scheduled appointment. After chatting for a bit, he requested a tour of the house and the proposed addition site. As we meandered through the house and yard, eventually arriving at the dining room, he too stopped in front of the oil painting and its damaged frame. *Here we go,* I thought. Initially looking at the painting from a distance, he then drew in close, stooping to find a signature. After a brief period of silence and the exchange of a few questions and comments about the portrait, he stepped back once again. "It's beautiful," he said, his eyes darting from painting, to frame, and back, " . . . stunning."

We hired him. But not because he had flattered us. We hired him because he got it. Rather than seeing the frame as a distraction, he had obviously seen it was an integral part of the portrait's beauty. No, the movers had not dropped it. Time and life had caressed it with their weathered hands, bestowing on it a grace that could only be fully seen and understood with the heart. If this architect could appreciate the rugged beauty of our painting, perhaps he would honor the beauty of our old home.

The heart's encounter with God's character is really no different. Our imaginations must be given the freedom to soar beyond the confines of our faith's cosmetic frames and into a place where we see—perhaps for the first time—that God's beauty is at once fierce and wonderful, thunderous and quiet, heartbreaking and exhilarating. When we look into God's being we must be willing to see what is there, not just those things about God that are familiar or appropriate to what I believe are my real concerns.

In his engaging book *How to Read a Poem,* Edward Hirsch describes the impact of poetry in his life as "a transfiguring passion . . . a force beyond the confines of the conscious self."[1] Intimacy with God is, in many ways, similar to Hirsch's bond with poetry. To know God is to be transfigured by him, not just amused or entertained. And this transfiguring often occurs in ways grasped only by our visceral awareness.

There are many times when the Christian will sense only that God is on the move; to where and for what purpose he won't immediately know. For a time, all he will know is that there is at work in him a force beyond his conscious awareness.

And he knows that this force is the force of God's Spirit, because it doesn't allow him to dodge or justify. It jostles him, tosses him about, renders him transparent, sometimes heaving him to shore like a surf-pounded jellyfish with no blustering sting left in him. He knows that these severe mercies are from God because who else but God would love him enough to shake him from his self-deceptions.

To see God in this way, however, is sometimes as frightening as it is breathtaking. And yet we can never know God's heart until we come to prefer authenticity and truth over familiarity.

So how will we recognize this kind of beauty when we see it? How do we suspend our insecurities and prejudices—our expectations of what God's portrait is supposed to look like—so we might approach him in a less fettered way?

As an initial exercise in accessing this refreshingly imaginative spirit, picture in your mind's eye a horse. What do you see? Perhaps it's a painted pony grazing in a meadow of sunflowers and honeybees. Or maybe it's tall and proud like one in an old English painting, with an equally tall and proud man sitting on its back wearing a red coat with large, black buttons, and holding a stiff leather crop. Or maybe it's something substantially different. Here is C. S. Lewis's image of a horse:

> *As it grew it changed. Its hinder parts grew rounder.*
> *The tail, still flickering, became a tail of hair that*
> *flickered between huge and glossy buttocks.*
> *Suddenly, I started back, rubbing my eyes. What*
> *stood before me was the greatest stallion I have ever*
> *seen, silvery white but with mane and tail of gold. It*
> *was smooth and shining, rippled with swells of flesh*
> *and muscle, whinnying and stamping with its hoofs.*
> *At each stamp the land shook and the trees dindled.[2]*

Now there's a horse! This horse has no interest in posing. To be simply in its presence is to be swept away into its very being. To ride on its powerful back, a privilege beyond imagination.

What have we done with the God whose love is so bold, whose presence is so intimate, whose laughter, joy, and pain are so eternally endemic to his character that we can smell his breath, see the steam rising from his torso, feel his firm but gentle hand on the nape of our necks? We have sanitized and homogenized him. Stripped of all mystery, the freshly gilded frame again shimmers and the beatific god contained within is safely corralled.

It is unfortunate how modern faith seems more often concerned with how to secure God to its religiously erudite moorings than with how to appreciate his breathtaking nature. It is no wonder that others often experience us as the smug, bitter ones, the anything-but-loving-and-joyful ones. It is to our great shame that the unsightly tread marks of our spiritual machinations often track across the bleeding back of the very Savior we profess to serve.

Even so, God's light shines through. One effect of our efforts to tame our faith's (and, by extension, our life's) mysteries is a renewed, intuitive longing for what is untamed. We've had our fill of grand solutions with short-lived staying power. We crave any morsel of authentic faith we can find.

EYES WIDE OPEN

What if we became so infused, so saturated with the nature and being of God himself that we became known as the passionate ones, the creative ones, the ones who are able to imagine a life and a God so much bigger than the one currently installed in the culture of Right Christian Living? What if we were passionate in our love, our forgiveness, our pain, our honest wrestling with the mysteries, betrayals, and joys of life?

Here's how I think we might begin to engage God in this way:

Acknowledge the Burning Heart

In Luke 24, we find one of the most revealing and instructive passages in all of Scripture. The setting is the road from Jerusalem to Emmaus, and the initial players are two disciples, Cleopas and an unnamed companion. As the scene opens we find the two travelers in animated discussion about recent events. Rumor has it that some had actually seen a "risen" Christ. But how could this be? How could all of the unfortunate events of the past few weeks possibly yield such an unimaginably wonderful result, anyway? How dare these rumormongers fan such an emotion-laden flame!

Mid-discussion they are joined by a stranger. One imagines a gradual joining of strides and words as the stranger inquires into the nature of their discussion. "Are you the only one who hasn't heard?" they ask. "Heard what?" replies the stranger. And so the exchange quickens as the disciples unload their hearts, and the strangely authoritative fellow walking beside them gives a history lesson they will never forget.

Arriving at their destination, the stranger indicates that he will travel on without them. "Won't you stay with us?" they ask. He accepts their invitation. But it is not until they have settled around the evening meal that he opens the eyes of their understanding and, in so doing, reveals himself.

It is Christ! They are stunned. Then he disappears. "Didn't our hearts burn within us as he spoke to us on the road?" they reflect. I can easily hear them also saying, "How is it possible that he was with us the whole time and we didn't even know it!" In this account's final scene, we find them in the temple, basking in the wonder of all that has just happened.

Several things strike me about this encounter.

First, often we too "sense" God within our hearts before we are aware it is God who speaks and walks with us. In this way, our affections for God more naturally reflect the honest emotions of a child's heart than they do the more deliberate research of a Bible scholar. We must be open to our heart's prodding. Our heart often reveals to us what our mind can't.

Theological study has its place. But it can also subdue

the burning heart. If our theology buffers us from our some-what impulsive, touchy-feely hearts, then it's a sure bet we will never be alert enough to invite the stranger into our home. "Good talking with you," we'll say. "Appreciate your exceptional insights. . . . Have a nice trip."

The second thing that strikes me in this passage is how important it is to Christ that the disciples see him in a fresh, new way. Had he instantly revealed himself to them while on the road as the very literal, physical Christ they knew—the way he looked, his tone of voice, the smell of his cloak, his sun-chafed cheeks—these cues would have, paradoxically, distracted them from his more essential being.

"I burn most passionately in your heart," he seemed to be saying. "I want to be even more alive to you *there* than I was in the life we shared when I spoke and lived among you in the flesh. I am so much more than what you can see and touch. Allow my Spirit to teach you this."

I am just now beginning to hear this stranger's voice. And I know I'm not the only one who hears it. I believe it is the voice of a renegade entreating us to take a chance, to come share in his resurrected life in a way far more adven-turous than the one we have known to this point.

As it was for the two disciples, there are those moments—the near misses—when we sense this stranger walking next to us on our well-traveled path. Gently placing his hand on our arm, he leans toward us, whispering words that sound foreign—deep, haunting words: "There is more," he says. "Within this journey of faith are many rich and mysterious trails and adventures. Let me tell you the story one more time. Let me restore your spiritual hearing. Let me remind you who I most essentially am."

For a moment—this moment sometimes lasting a lifetime—we feel the blood run hot in our veins. Like Cleopas and his companion we find ourselves arrested by a wonderful something—or a wonderful some*one*—desiring our attention. "Isn't my heart burning within me?" we echo. At that moment we are keenly inspired and refreshed. We want to forsake everything. We want to test the muscles in our legs, feel the cool sweat of life on our brow. We are at once stirred and shaken by the stranger's words. Then, like an echo in a distant canyon, another voice—the voice of "the Christian life as we've come to know it"—calls us back from our foolishness: "Hey, let's go! We've got to trudge up and down the trail, you know."

"Yes, right," we say, reeling from our all-too-close encounter with the living God. "What was I thinking? I nearly lost the ground I have been so obediently gaining."

Relieved to be rescued from the daring impulse to forfeit our place in line in order to follow the stranger down some untrodden path, we resume the familiar march . . . up and down . . . up and down . . . once again narrowly escaping a transformational opportunity.

Unlike the disciples on the Emmaus road, we rarely, if ever, make it to dinner. We rarely sit down to an eye-opening feast with Christ.

Think Downside Up

In addition to acknowledging the burning heart, a second, open-hearted way to hear God's voice afresh is to think downside up.

We plant the seed of an imaginative faith when we begin to understand that the daily downs of living are actually the transformational fodder for the imaginative life. They are the upside as far as our being transformed into the image of Christ is concerned. As James 1:2 urges ("consider it pure joy"), we are to plumb the riches within these challenges instead of detesting and running from them.

It is at times unfortunate that the personal lay testimonies most often shared from the pre-sermon pulpit are nearly always of the "victory" sort. Don't get me wrong—victory is good. It has biblical precedent. I love it when the good guys win. But the victories extolled are too often victories *over* instead of victories *within*. These sorts of victories have a hollow ring to them. They are like the tale of a ship in foggy weather that almost runs aground but is warned off at the last possible moment by a saving lighthouse beam. Threat perceived, threat deterred, all is well.

One of the few times I've ever wept for joy was while reading Anne Lamott's *Traveling Mercies*. What my gut responds to in her writing is the unshakable impression that she is not just "showing up" (à la Woody Allen), but that she is bringing an accessibility of heart and soul with her to the table. Her poignant quips, "God loves you just the way you are, but he loves you too much to let you stay like this," and "I don't know what the future holds but I know who holds the future"[3]—though seemingly trite—reveal a heart exposed to God. They tell me that she understands the relentless transformational nature of an evolving faith and that she acknowledges the sometimes mysterious wisdom of God's engagement with this world.

As she is being wooed and challenged by a Christ who best knows her many burdens, Lamott lacks pretension. She reminds me of the newly sighted blind man's response in John 9:25 to the arrogant spiritual leaders as they questioned him about the one who had healed him: "One thing I do know. I was blind, but now I see!"

God bless the visual purity of the religiously unsophisticated!

Embrace a Conversion to Transformation

As you are aware by now, one of this book's central themes is that the perfecting of faith is achieved not through our perfectionistic efforts, but through our malleability to God's transforming purposes. Too often we think of transformation as the process of purging life's challenges and interruptions. But nothing could be further from the truth. The wise Elihu says to Job: "But those who suffer he delivers *in* their suffering; he speaks to them *in* their affliction" (Job 36:15, emphasis added).

Transformation is the dynamic, ongoing coalescence— not the sorting and selective expunging—of sorrow, certainty, pain, love, mystery, truth, humility, victory, that issues in what we refer to as "our life in Christ."

A third way to begin seeing God through fresh eyes, then, is to realize that an important role of God's Spirit is to help wean us from the conversion *event* to the transformation *process*. In the same manner that each stage of building a house is simultaneously the fruition of the stage that came before it and the foundation for the one that comes after, each transformation of the self is never final. It is both fruit and seed.

This understanding of transformation as process lies at the very core of the imaginative spirit. To take it even one step further, as we begin to imagine the unlimited range of

God's creativity, we will come to see that our conversion is not entirely our conversion. God is continually in the process of converting us—from our will to his way; from our fear to his assurance; from our efforts to his sufficiency; from our pursuit of the Christian life to an abandonment to his life within us.

It is into God's very nature that we are being transformed, and this transformation almost never occurs in the fantastic manner that we often equate with spiritual conversion. Rather it is nearly always an evolving, brick-and-mortar endeavor.

I remember once hearing a sportscaster's interview with a professional NFL kicker. He asked the player if he had any inspirational advice he wanted to pass on to other aspiring kickers. "Trim your toenails," he replied, "then go out and kick the ball."

GOING HOME TO A PLACE
WE'VE NEVER BEEN BEFORE

Moving more deeply into our transformation—into that place where we can begin to imagine the unlimited nature of God's creativity—requires a symphonic alertness to the knowable, the sense-able, and the mysterious. For the imaginative Christian, this more improvisational state of being is her home, the place where she is most intimately connected to all that she loves and values. It is where she sees that even in the midst of the certainty, mystery, fragmentation, and wholeness that most truly define her life in Christ (which we will discuss thoroughly in part 2), God is undeniably with her, supplying refreshment from the most unlikely sources.

We must never lose sight of the fact that always present in our lives is a God who is so much greater than our circumstances. The ability to remain faithful ("not lose heart," 2 Corinthians 4:16) in this journey of transformation as it engages these circumstances—whatever they may be—is the miracle that Christ's victory has won.

chapter 3

IMAGINING THE PRESENT

"I have been anxious . . . to stand on the meeting
of two eternities, the past and the future, which is
precisely the present moment; to toe that line."
HENRY DAVID THOREAU, *Walden*

I sit here like the young, freckle-faced fisherman in a Norman Rockwell painting, my bare feet dangling over the edge of the brick patio floor of my old home, pondering the gaping hole that plummets about a story and a half beneath my toes.

Earlier I saw my neighbor, Andy, staring blankly over our shared fence into the great abyss that was once his neighbor's yard. When he regains consciousness, I'll remind him that the completed addition will be roughly half of what the excavation suggests.

Still, it's one giant hole!

The seven-year-old boy living two houses to the north asked me why we were building another house so close to the one we already have.

And to think it all started with a sputtering, flame-throwing oven. How simple it would have been just to replace the thing for a grand or so. Instead we will soon have an addition that could easily house a truckload of ovens.

But in this adventure—this process of tearing down and building up, of uncovering and concealing, of losing and gaining—there is at play some compellingly primitive process.

It's as if by sitting here, staring into this hole, I unearth my life.

It was on a frigid night just two Aprils ago that I lay in the thick, damp grass once carpeting this space, holding in my arms for the last breaths of her life our exhausted, cancer-ridden dog, Shadow.

It was in this yard that a legion of family and friends gathered three years ago to celebrate our daughter's first birthday. The spark of her being waited patiently inside her mother's womb for forty years—numerous infertility treatments and marriage trials spawned by the ordeal—before changing us forever with the miracle of her birth. Standing on this very patio I had intended to give a rousing speech to our backyard guests regarding the unfathomable gift of a child's life. Instead the only words I could manage were "I'm so grateful."

It was while sitting with my feet propped on this patio's circular table one glorious autumn afternoon that I first acknowledged my deep passion for writing. In a flurry of thought soon thereafter, I scribbled on a coffee-stained legal pad the words: "for religion I have little affection . . . it is Christ that I love" and, in so doing, rediscovered the One who had been patiently waiting for me to return to my heart. Through my inadequacies as a husband, father, brother, and son, God had mercifully shown me that my tower of principled Right Christian Living was fog-bound. For all of its imposing presence, it had come to offer no view beyond its own walls.

So, much more than nostalgic indulgence, it now occurs to me that, in probing my past, I find the present. In recalling Shadow's wet, matted fur pressed against my frozen cheeks, in reliving a gratitude more experienced than spoken, in recalling a few words crystallizing the essence of a long desert journey, I encounter my life's most certain truth: God with me; God *always* with me.

As I sit here nursing the same spiritual limp as every other living soul, watching the iron fangs of a brute machine reveal the fertile soil buried in my backyard, I find hope in transformation. I see water gushing forth from stone.

THE PRESENT DEFINED

The Present Present

In what is certainly one of Christianity's great ironies, the promise of heaven and the victory of the cross loom so imposingly (and rightfully so) over our faith's horizon that we are tempted to forsake the present in deference to the great futuristic vision that heaven and the cross inspire within us. Accordingly, we are prone to hear Christ's words in John: "In this world you will have tribulation; but be of good cheer, I have overcome the world" (16:33, NKJV) as pertaining to a joyful manifestation of the cross yet to be realized.

And we can hardly be faulted for hearing it this way because, after all, just look at the tumbled lives we live on this careening planet. Certainly, nothing good can come out of *this* Nazareth!

There is something innately uncomfortable about *now*. To look at how most of us live, one would have to conclude that we would rather be living anywhere else but in the present. It's as if we consider the present to be no more than a staging area from which we must either wrestle our past or yearn our future.

Yes, the abundant life must surely be the future one, the one in which all evil is finally purged and God's kingdom

reigns supreme. If we can all hang on just a little longer
. . . yes, just a little longer.

But then, out of the blue comes another one of those
nagging questions: Is it possible that this *present* life (the
one we live at this moment) *is* the promised, abundant one?
Not: Is it possible for this life to eventually *become* the abundant life, but rather: Is it *now* the abundant one?

To answer no is to say that Christ's death and resurrection have only made it possible for us to *get* somewhere—
"getting" (that is, doing, performing, positioning) being the
operative word—and this "somewhere" has virtually no
relationship to where we are now. Accordingly, the
Christian life then becomes the quintessential treasure hunt,
with the Bible being the map showing the way and the hunt
being the trail we blaze through life's tangled, menacing forest to get to wherever "somewhere" is.

Oh, the spiritual troops we marshal and the steely
blades of dogma we hone in our exasperation to procure an
abundance we already have!

But just as a child who is already human grows *into* her
humanity we too grow *into* the abundance of our redeemed
lives. We don't grow *toward* Christ, but rather *in* him.

So is it possible that *this* is the abundant life? I believe
the answer is yes. I believe that God's life-giving presence
flows forth—even now, even when I can't see it and even

when I may choose not to avail myself of it—from this broken and weathered stone called my present life.

The Eternal Present

Having realized this, it would be misleading to define the present only as "now." For one who lives in the present is not necessarily one who lives *for this moment,* but rather, one who *brings to this moment* an eternal perspective. I know I am living fully in the present when I can see the eternal past and the eternal future from where I stand.

Thus I know I am most present when I am able to suspend my busyness long enough to see in my loved one's face the pain of her wounds, the joys of her personal redemptions. I know I am living most fully in the present when I can see and feel in this moment those things from which the anesthetizing noise of my life and my fears shield me.

One morning before heading into the office, about a year after Shadow died, I was driving our daughter, Paige, to day care. I was battling traffic and battling my attitude as our usual three-lane-wide, metal snake slithered west on Eighteenth Avenue into downtown Denver. From an elevated perch in her snazzy Eddie Bauer car seat, Paige could see a man with a black dog crossing one of the outlying parking lots just east of the Brown Palace Hotel. "Daddy," she said, more to herself than to me, "I sure miss Shadow."

"I do too, Paige," I replied. "I do too."

After a lengthy silence she again said, "Daddy"—this time with the eager tone of someone who just had a great idea and wanted to test it out.

"Yes?" I responded.

"Umm . . . umm . . . could we maybe someday have heaven here?" she asked.

I suddenly felt that same pain in my throat that I had as a child at the end of *Lassie Come Home* when Timmy is burying Lassie's toys—his heart tearing apart—but then, hearing a familiar bark, he turns to see his long-lost companion bounding over the hill and into his arms. Oh, what pain; oh, what joy!

Could we maybe someday have heaven here? What a question. And yet, isn't this the question most of us are really asking? Lord, could we maybe someday see the Promised Land? Could I maybe have my dog back with me for a little while? Could I please have some financial freedom—some success in my company or, at least, in my marriage? Okay, then, how about something for someone else, like a loving spouse for my son, good health for my aging mother, or just a little bread and water for the starving? Could we maybe, someday, have heaven here?

It *is* here, says Christ. It's right here in the scarred cavity in my side—put your finger here and see. It's right here in the blind man's stolen sight, the lame man's withered legs, the tiny mustard seed, the birds of the air, and the belly of a whale. You think there is anything I can't see and don't know? Think again. Believe me, I know better than anyone what and where heaven is, and, make no mistake, it is here in abundance. Pray for eyes to see and ears to hear.

Yes, says Jesus, pray and pay attention.

To live our lives in the memory of what was, or in the anticipation of what will be, is to live in a netherworld, a world floating just slightly behind or ahead of us. The more common word for this state of being—this absence from the present—is *distracted*. And the antidote to distraction is attention to what is.

The Particular Present

In her Pulitzer Prize-winning book, *Pilgrim at Tinker Creek*, Annie Dillard—borrowing from Stephen Graham's image of a "great door"—says, "I discover that [the great door] . . . opened on time: Where else? That Christ's incarnation occurred improbably, ridiculously, at such-and-such a time, into such-and-such a place, is referred to—with great sincerity even among believers—as "the scandal of particularity."[1]

I think Dillard has her finger on a truth that often escapes us. The great door of God's eternal purposes—of his very being—opens not only on time, but on *this* time. Although his glorious image is certainly reflected in the children of the world, or the grandeur of the forests and fields, or the universe's spinning galaxies, the Christian message is that God chooses to fully reveal himself in *this* child who lives in *this* town in *this* country and is hung on *this* tree, is buried in *this* tomb, and, finally, reveals to *these* people his resurrected glory.

It is difficult to imagine such a big God indwelling such small, *particular* spaces as these. And it is bothersome. It's like having royalty knocking on one's door, requesting to stay the night and use one's shower and toilet. Yikes! To imagine that God indwells the particular present (this moment) has the same uncomfortable feel about it. It's far easier to admire (or worship, as the case may be) from a distance. Far easier to speak of God in general terms. Far more comfortable to leave royalty to their palaces and limousines.

I'll never forget the first time I saw the Godfather of Soul, James Brown, perform on the Ed Sullivan Show: "And here he ish . . . on our shtage . . . James Brown!" The funky horns and bass fire up. Standing near the back of the stage, just beyond the reach of the glaring lights, in an ethereal atmosphere of diffused light and stage fog, stands a caped, lit stick of dynamite in the dark, athletic guise of James Brown. From stage left another man emerges. Lifting the shimmering silk cape from the legend's shoulders, he fades into the darkness just as quickly as he had appeared. Then suddenly, Brown hits center stage. The lights pop with intensity. With rivulets of sweat streaking down his face, he not so much sings as preaches. He's here to tell you that Papa does, indeed, have a brand new bag and that any other thought ain't worth squat—at least not for the next three minutes.

How could such a raspy voice sound so good? How can he possibly hit that high-pitched "Ohww," do the splits, and remember the words, all at the same time? As the brass's emphatic, staccatoed bursts begin to taper—daht, daht . . . dahta dah daht—the man from stage left reappears. Attempting to recloak the singer, he is initially rebuffed. In a state of apparent delirium and exhaustion, however, Brown finally accepts the cape and allows the man to lead him from the stage. The fog, the sound, the energy, hang in the air. Ed Shullivan is shpeechlesh. James Brown came— and definitely conquered. And don't you forget it!

Now, isn't the "royal" model precisely this? The great one, accompanied by celestial haze and a symphony of angel wings, appears on our humble stage, performs his magic, and is then spirited away before we can figure out what happened. That's how it works; that's how the appropriate distance—and the appropriate degree of mesmerizing stupor—is maintained. That's how royalty maintain their royal image.

God is supposed to hide himself in the drama. Perhaps he could foster a whole new spiritual vocabulary in which we who sit in the Sunday-morning pews could become even more lost and confused than we already are. Words like *post-tribulation* and *soteriological,* phrases like "raised up," "consumed by the fire of our wanton desires," and— well, why not?—"Papa's got a brand new bag" are very helpful in this regard. Anything to keep us distracted from the fact that God loves us, knows us intimately, and is far more interested in our brokenness and joy, and in the authenticity of our love for others than he is in our denominational bearings and intricate theological understandings.

But apparently, the God of the universe doesn't understand this. He's got it all wrong. He's far too personal. He could use a consultation with Brown's agent.

Which brings us back to the particularity of God's presence in this world. Have you ever wondered why Christ— let's say, during the three years preceding his death and resurrection—didn't just wave a magic wand or something and heal the people's ills in one fell swoop? Why did he even bother to address their requests on such a personal level? Why did he glob spit and mud on one man's sightless eyes, tell another to take a dip in the pool, and instruct yet another to stretch out his leprous hands and be healed? It's because the physical healing was never the point. The real issue was then—and to this day, remains—the broken-hearted soul, the wounded spirit, the estranged relationship *behind* the eyes, the legs, the hands.

And so it is with us.

God is intensely and unshakably interested and active in the spiritual journeys on which our life circumstances take us. He knows the *particular* spiritual nuances involved in one's recovery from the loss of a child; another's *particular* emotional struggle with the demise of a marriage and the feelings of abandonment and mistrust of love that ensue; another's *particular* spiritual and physical exhaustion from battling cancer or diabetes.

God may sometimes choose to heal a physical wound because he knows something we don't about its relationship to the greater, more important healing of the soul. Or—for the same reason—he might say to us, as he did to the apostle Paul, "My grace is sufficient" (2 Corinthians 12:9).

Either way, we must remain open to the spiritual truth that a thing does not have to be restored for it to be redeemed. More often than not, the abundance we seek will be found *within the imperfect particularities* of our lives. To seek for it elsewhere is to seek for something other than God.

Eternal Perspective in the Particulars of Life

So, how do we learn to bring an eternal perspective to the present particulars of our lives? Being the solutions-oriented people that we are, we will tend to look for a handy technique or a system. But what we really need is a shift in our thinking. To begin to see how it could possibly be true that this life we now live is the blessed, abundant one, here are a few thoughts on how to shift our way of thinking.

Present-Mindedness

Those who desire to live in a more present-minded fashion might find the following qualities to be of help. The present-minded person:

- *Likes a good mystery*—Can distinguish between the pursuit of truth and the pursuit of answers.
- *Has time*—Understands that the present is the context for the adventure of faith.
- *Can pat her head and rub her stomach at the same time*—Can entertain the paradoxes of faith without being compelled to reconcile them.
- *Knows what "emotional patina" is*—Can value and access the more intuitive emotional life and confidently traverse the path between intellectual and emotional knowing.

- *Is not agenda-loaded*—Understands that the people and life around him are his compatriots, not his projects.
- *Can hear beyond the sound of words*—Is not so caught up with and dependent on certain catch-phrases of Christian faith that she cannot discern the pulse and intent of a person's heart—whether that person is Christian or not.

To place one's hope fully in God is to trust that he is fully here. It is to imagine that God's sustenance is trapped in neither the past nor the future. God is here with you. Now.

Can you imagine?

Part Two

THE
EYES
OF
FAITH

chapter 4

SEEING CERTAINTY

The beginning of wisdom is to get you a roof.
WEST AFRICAN PROVERB

The fear of the LORD is the beginning of wisdom.
PSALM 111:10

———⁓———

s we begin this section on the eyes of faith, it
will be helpful to briefly recount the Israelites'
journey through the desert.

As you recall, the people are complaining to Moses
because they feel God is not adequately caring for them.
"When he struck the rock, water gushed out, and streams
flowed abundantly," they said, adding, "But can he also give
us food? Can he supply meat for his people?" (Psalm 78:20).

Yes, God had given them water from stone. And we

know they had received their meat and bread. At every turn the Israelites were sustained, led, protected, and generally fussed over by God himself. But it wasn't enough.

So when Moses is slow in returning from Mount Sinai, they seize the opportunity to get control of the situation. "Come," they say to Aaron, "make us gods who will go before us" (Exodus 32:1). The gold is gathered and the golden calf forged.

And God is angry.

He essentially tells Moses, "I've had it with these stiff-necked people. They just don't get it."

And neither do we. We too are stiff-necked people. In our impatience for results, we try to force God's hand. If he won't care for us in a way that makes sense to us, then we'll create a snappy program—a culture of Right Christian Living—that will.

So what is it that neither the Israelites nor today's church gets? What is it we just can't see?

In this and the next three chapters I will suggest that we cannot see because we are not used to shifting our eyes from a focus on the present to a gaze at the eternal—and back again—with any degree of ease. We need a pilgrim's skill of watching the stony path under our feet while also keeping our eyes on the horizon. To help us acquire this skill, I suggest we need four lenses, four ways of seeing that will help us rethink our life of faith. They are: certainty, mystery, fragmentation, and wholeness.

What do these things have to do with how we are trading a passion for God with the lentil stew of Right Christian Living? Let's begin with certainty, and see.

THE CERTAIN THING

Lost about ten years ago in our move from cottage to colonial, my senior class yearbook was expressively graffitied with the exuberant well-wishes of my classmates. One of the most common entries, of course, was the catchall sentiment, "You're a really great guy! Don't ever change!"

There is something about the predictable, the thoroughly knowable person or thing, that brings us comfort. Once we become oriented to who, what, where, why, and when a certain thing is, we want it concretized. We want to know that we can always count on it, that it "won't ever change." We want to be in control.

So when we read in Hebrews 13:8 about Christ never changing, that he is "the same yesterday and today and forever," we are greatly comforted. What relief to know that what we see is what we get.

But therein lies a tragic but common mistake we make regarding our view of Christ and, consequently, our faith: we

assume that what we see of Christ through our finite per-
ceptions is all there is to see. We assume that if Christ does
a thing a certain way once, he will do it that same way in the
future. We confuse same *action* with same *character*. In so
doing, we dodge the real issue—the cultivation of an abid-
ing trust in God—in favor of our peevish doubts about his
ability or willingness to meet our expectations for the future.

The instinct to make a thing predictable, to collar it, is a
difficult one to shake. It is certainly important to get our theology straight, to gain the most accurate understanding we can
of who God is and how our lives in him are to be lived. But
we must not then go on to assume that in clarifying our theology, we can also put God in the box of our expectations.

Dependability Versus Predictability

So, what does Scripture mean when it tells us that we can
count on Christ to remain the same—yesterday, today, and
forever? I think it is telling us that we can depend on his solid
nature. What we can count on is that his actions will *always*
reflect his tenacious love, even if that reflection gives the
impression of a savior who doesn't care, is impotent to act,
or has anything but our best interests in mind. Christ's freedom to act within the unlimited sphere and unfathomable
creativity of his love is the most essential unchanging thing
about him.

Thus he may choose *not* to heal, *not* to unleash the heavenly justice posse on the world's immediate evils, *not* to grant us that new job or long-awaited child as a reward for our faithful prayers and service.

It is in the light of Christ's freedom to love us in ways that sometimes make sense—and sometimes don't—that the imaginative Christian comes to count not on Christ's predictability, but on his innate goodness; not on a spiritualized image of who she wants Christ to be, but on the sustaining intimacy of his presence. This is what imaginative faith begins to see.

To be sure, the one thing we can count on with Christ is that he will remain forever, unchangingly, our loving Lord. We have the unshakable, objective reality of the cross, forever driven into the ground of history.

For several years I've maintained a counseling office in downtown Denver's quaint and historic Grant Street Mansion. And every morning—at precisely 9:55—a slightly disheveled, gray-haired whistler has come shuffling past my garden-level window. With his tune nearly engulfed by the low, dull hum of passing cars and buses, however, I've only been able to discern *that*—not *what*—he is whistling.

Fortunately, I was sitting one day with a client who knows my quirks even better than I know his, and who was familiar with the whistler's morning routine, when a most unusual thing happened. At 9:55 the whistler came shuffling past my window . . . singing! I interrupted my client mid-sentence (I'm not kidding about this) and said, "He's singing! The whistler is singing!" After explaining to my client that the whistler had never sung before and that it had caught me off guard, we resumed the session.

But I remained hopelessly distracted. And I conceived a plan. A deceptive, diabolical plan. Tomorrow, before my 10:00 session, I would buy a Sprite from the pop machine, go lean against the stone wall bordering the sidewalk, and wait for the whistler to show himself. Then, in the guise of a therapist enjoying a brief respite from his work, I would pounce. "Why were you singing yesterday?" I'd ask. "What would possess you to change the routine? Give an account of yourself!" I'd demand.

And that (with only a few minor modifications in delivery) is precisely what I did.

And here is the account he gave: "It's April."

What? I thought. It's *April?* What does that have to do with anything? Caught off guard yet again, all I could manage in reply was a feeble, "Of course . . . have a good day."

And to this day I wonder what April could possibly have to do with singing and why, to the whistler, the connection was so self-evident. "It's April," he had said, so matter-of-factly.

Upon hearing this story some time later, a good friend put it all in perspective: "Well, one thing's for sure," she said, "the whistler loves music."

And maybe that's the real point, after all. Either whistling or singing, the whistler's essential spirit remains consistent. I can count on him—April or not—to be caught up in song.

And so it is with Christ. Whether walking beside us on a dusty road, weeping at our tombs, laughing with our children, impaled with spikes to a cross—yes, even temporarily staving off evil or healing the sick with a mere touch—Christ's character remains intact. He is unchanging. His ways are not our ways. It's April. And to him, it makes all the sense in the world because he has borne the world's full weight on his back and has suffocated in the stench and death of hell's rankest bowels.

No, he's not predictable. But he's unfathomably, most certainly, dependable. He's been there. He knows what he's doing. We can count on it.

Immanence Versus Transcendence

I don't know if it's because of our society's obsession with power and position or simply the modern penchant for compartmentalizing, but we Christians have become enthralled with the image of a God who is transcendent, who sits outside it all and cracks the whip, dispenses justice, and gives raises and bonuses to the worthy.

A celestial Batman, of sorts. Hiding, completely unde-tected and not wanting to be detected, in Gotham's inner sanctums. In the City but not of it. Ever scanning the heav-ens, waiting for the downtroddens' Batlight to appear in the clouds, summoning him to come fight the good fight.

The thought that God would inhabit both spiritual and physical dimensions of his creation, that he would surf the veinal highways of our bodies, smell what we smell, under-stand our arousals, our misgivings, our yearnings and joys, causes us to break out in a self-conscious sweat. We cer-tainly want God to know us . . . but not *that* intimately.

For just a moment I'd like to take us on a brief excur-sion. All it will require is an openness of spirit and a little imagination.

You're lying on the back porch lounge, watching the sprinkler douse the lawn and the unsuspecting dog. Or you're in that old leather chair in the study, next to the book-case stocked with your favorite reads. Perhaps you're in an airplane terminal or in the Rover's passenger seat on your way to a family getaway in the mountains. Or you're just hanging out in the breakfast nook on a rare lazy Saturday.

Wherever you are physically planted at this moment, a kind and gracious voice enters the space. "Hello. May I sit with you?" it asks. You are not startled. You have heard

Christ's voice before. You hear it mostly with your heart.

"Yes, please," you respond.

"How is it with your soul?" he asks.

"Well, you know . . . just hangin' in there. Taking it as it comes."

"I see. And that pain in your shoulder?" he continues.

"Glad you asked," you respond. "Maybe you'd like to help out a little with that."

"May I touch your shoulder?" he asks.

"Certainly," you respond. "I could sure use a good, old-fashioned healing with this thing."

"I said nothing about healing it. I asked only to touch it, to put my hand on it."

At this point you're confused. Why would Christ want to touch your shoulder if he didn't intend to heal it? Why else would he possibly want to touch it? You're also a little angry. Healing is what he's about. Why doesn't he just step up and do his job?

Then it hits you: he'll heal it in a minute. He just needs to get the spiritual dynamics in order first. "Oh, of course. It's especially bothersome right here by this bone," you say.

He smiles, turns his body square to yours. "May I enter your pain?" he asks.

Finally! Christ will reach into your shoulder, do his thing, and be on his way. "Of course," you say.

"I'm not sure you understand," he responds. "I'd like to enter your pain, become a part of it. Feel its heat and poison. Somewhere in your flesh a part of your soul is trapped. If in freeing your soul your shoulder is healed as well, then so be it. But the physical healing isn't necessary. What I'm asking is if you will allow me, through the fire in your flesh, to enter your deeper pain."

And this is where the various Christian camps begin hoisting their respective banners. It would never go that far, says one camp. If one's request for healing harbored no secret doubts, then one would be healed. God's desire is to heal us; the problem is our lack of faith, not his will to heal. Just a minute, says another. How do you know that the voice you hear is truly God's? Maybe it's your own subconscious desires—your own psychological introjections. You're both wrong, says a third. Pain and suffering are God's means of getting our attention. Why are you so intent on getting rid of them? And all three have Scripture to back up their view.

And Christ asks you, yet again, "May I enter your pain?"

Paralyzed with indecision, you avert your eyes. Silence returns.

If God is not indelibly in our pain, if he is not in our suffering, then where is he? His Batmobile? Maybe down the block a piece? Gone to lunch . . . be back at 1:00? Perhaps he is like the castaway girl in the Disney classic *Swiss Family Robinson,* standing transcendentally on dry ground, trying with a stick to fish the frightened zebra out of the quicksand.

"God is in the details," said the architect Ludwig Mies van der Rohe. Although he meant it in reference to the considered application of certain architectural elements, he has no idea how literally true his statement is. God is truly *in* the details of every part of our lives. He inhabits them.

Can you imagine that God indwells your brokenness as well as your joy? That he literally suffers with you and that this pain and suffering make up only the current context, not the final word, of your life?

Can you imagine a thoroughly immanent God? Can you imagine Christ in your suffering with you, or is he your Christ only if and when the suffering goes away?

Redemption Versus Protection

One of my clients said it best. In reference to his wife's affair and the resulting tide of turmoil and pain, he remarked, "As a Christian, one would expect a certain degree of protection."

Yes, one would. What good is a god who sits casually by while his loved ones' lives are torn asunder? What good is a god who doesn't keep us safe?

With the life of God himself flowing in us, we must certainly have access to a measure of protection that others don't have. So why do we still bleed when cut? Why do we wreck our cars, mourn our dead children, suffer injustice and infidelity, feel our bones ache? Where's the bulletproof vest in the Christian survival kit?

For some reason we have come to think of God as the God of Prevention. A kind of firewall that stands between us and life's flames. But is it just possible that we are looking for God in all the wrong places? Is it just possible that while we are overly occupied with securing our bodies, relationships, and lifestyles, God is at work growing his eternal life within us?

I have come to believe that the physicality of our lives is actually quite neutral. It is the context of our spiritual transformation. As such, there is little that is certain about it.

We are to be good stewards of the physical/temporal realm, yes, but we are never to depend on it for our security. We are to give our very best to our marriages, our jobs, our children, our health, and our earth, but never with the idea in mind that—in so doing—we buy an unassailable life. What we *do* buy in our efforts is strength of character to face the stuff of life from which no one of us is exempt and a front row seat at the unfolding drama of God's redemptive work.

Yes, God sometimes protects, blesses, and speaks in

dramatic ways. But these aspects of our life in God pale in comparison to other characteristics of God's kingdom that are anything but dramatic. Training our ears on God's voice and our eyes on his face—even when it seems there is no one speaking and there is no face to be found—is by far the greater miracle, the greater evidence of God's life in us. This is a truly imaginative faith.

The Israelites questioned Moses: Is God here with us, or not? He was. And it wasn't enough.

Give us gold. Give us money in the bank. Give us the marriages, the passions, the children, the successes that will prove you are God. And in this attitude of entitlement our ears remain stopped, our eyes blind. In the search for our own version of certainty, we find nothing but emptiness.

Evidence of God's presence refuses to be collected and trophied like shells from the seashore. We encounter him *most* certainly in the steady, relentlessly unfolding redemption of our life's everyday circumstances, a redemption encountered mostly through faith.

FAITH

I typed the above word, then laughed. *Faith.*

Only God could pull this one off. Only God could require of us something we could never achieve. Only God could make central to our spirituality the most unattainable thing of all: faith. And what a stroke of genius it is. To require anything actually doable would seat us squarely on our own thrones, make us captains of our own ships. And doom us to ourselves.

And yet there is something innately strange about this faith. Although we can do nothing to muster it, it is only with our participation that its power is fully realized. Although we do not conceive it, it requires our spiritual womb for its birth.

And so here is the dilemma and, I think, the solution: If we seek faith, we find nothing; however, if we seek God, we find God . . . and that is all we need, because to truly see God is to see not only faith, but hope and love as well. This is important because we typically seek for a thing where we expect it to be found. And because God himself *is* the faith we seek, we will come up empty-handed if we search for it anywhere else.

Perhaps the following illustration will help us with this idea that God *is* our faith.

Just north of downtown Denver, on the north bank of the Platte River, is a large, flagship R.E.I. (Recreational Equipment Incorporated) compound—a purveyor of every imaginable recreational delight for out-of-doors enthusiasts.

When I need an especially mood-inducing, visually rich

place to write, the coffee shop at the south end of the century-old building is just the ticket. Only thirty feet beyond the coffee shop's ample windows, several of the Platte's small tributaries converge with gusto at Confluence Park, creating a bubbling, churning whitewater wonderland.

On one such writing excursion—while tapping away at my computer—I overheard through a large passageway between the coffee shop and the store, a clerk asking her customer who had just purchased a kayak, "So, are you going to put her in at the park?"

"Oh, no," he replied, "I'm making a coffee table out of it. A friend of mine has one, and it looks really cool."

We too often think of faith this same way—we want faith for faith's sake.

We are like Peter, proud of our purchase—that is, until it comes time for it to be truly tested. And then we, like Peter, realize the truth of it: it is not our faith, but rather our Christ who saves us. *"Lord,* save me!" cries Peter. In his desperation he sees that Christ himself is his faith. If Christ cannot save him, then nothing can.

"You of little faith," Christ says to Peter, "why did you doubt?" (Matthew 14:30-31).

Doubt what? Doubt Christ. Why did Peter doubt that Christ would sustain him? Because he lost sight of Christ's face and, in so doing, Peter lost sight of his faith.

Our search for faith can sometimes be this simple.

You want faith? Then look at the God who is with you. If you look until you can see his face, then there is no way you will come up empty-handed. You will come up, instead, with one of the most certain things of all: faith.

chapter 5

SEEING MYSTERY

But if no flying buttresses were to be built,
then how was the dome to be supported?
ROSS KING, *Brunelleschi's Dome*

———— ∽ ————

*O*ne of our family's great unsolved mysteries
involved the whereabouts of a certain gun and
holster set. I remember the gun as silver-barreled with genuine wood handles. The holster was hand-tooled leather
with robust stitching securing its trimmed edges. Although it
would have been one of the legendary toys of our waning
childhood on our miniature five-acre farm, this mother-of-all
cap guns never made it out of the box.

Intent on keeping it out of the destructive hands of a
certain visiting cousin, my brother dug a hole in the corner
of one of the horse stalls in the Big Black Shed, slid the

entire box in the hole, and tossed a little straw on top of the fresh mound of dirt for safekeeping. As our adolescent attention spans would have it, a month or so passed before we remembered the buried treasure.

And so began the search. For more than forty years now we have looked for it; we have dug, scraped, sifted, and trolled for it. By now, it is certainly worth at least as much as *Toy Story*'s Stinky Pete from the Woody's Roundup set. When it is finally found, I expect the Japanese toy connoisseurs— blank checks in hand—to come knocking.

But I am fairly certain this is one mystery that will never be solved. And yet, something tells me we have gotten far more reminiscent mileage out of the unfound gun and holster than we would have had my cousin never visited.

THE MYSTERY OF MYSTERY

I suppose one of the great mysteries of faith is why there have to be any mysteries at all. You would think that the cross took care of all that. You would think that Christ's victory would have dispelled the guesswork, the inexact science of faith. You would think our now-redeemed lives would reflect clear thoughts and pure actions. You would think we would never again lose our minds, our wills, or our treasures.

And yet mystery persists. In our eagerness to find answers,

both high and low deceive us: our high hopes and aspirations seem always to exceed our reach, and our despair is never so far beyond redemption as it might sometimes seem.

Mystery contains both the known and the unknown. In essence, mystery is spiritual truth that we can know only by revelation, but cannot fully understand. Like Abraham who "obeyed and went, even though he did not know where he was going,"[1] the passionate person learns to live in the tension caused by mystery.

But while some of us are at once driven and consumed by the very mystery we strain to grasp, others of us stagger about like wounded soldiers in a field of mines, praying that the next step won't be our last. This life of faith—this adventure of seeing our life in part, and yet trusting—is not for the weak-hearted.

Every year or so I get a call from a high school buddy and lifelong friend, Perry Bean. With no indication that what he is about to invite me to do has the strong potential of shortening—if not ending—the duration of our natural lives, he says, "Hey, Wayne . . . I'm thinking this summer of traversing from ocean to ocean over the Panama Strait. The guide won't speak English and we'll be slogging through mud and wading through snake-infested waters while pressing hand-hewn canoes over our heads. Want to come along?" Or, "How about joining me this winter in Minnesota. I'll be following a pack of wolves . . . sleeping in the wild, building snow caves and such . . . should be a good time."

Looking for a face-saving way to turn him down, I fan the calendar pages into the mouthpiece of my phone. "Darn it . . . busy that week . . . would love to go . . . send me pictures."

But now and then I rise to the challenge and join him for a more sedate adventure like climbing three fourteeners in one day, or, as I'm about to relate, spelunking one of the off-the-beaten-path underground tributaries of Colorado's Cave of the Winds.

Although this particular escapade was uncharacteristically legal and safe, it was nonetheless challenging. Leaving the standard cave tour to the easily intimidated, we at times found ourselves wading in darkness and flailing about on our stomachs like turtles making their way from sand to sea.

Several miles into the belly of the mountain, with all but the whites of our eyeballs layered thick in powdery cave dust, our guide turned to us and said, "While the good news is that we are now at the end of our adventure, the bad news is that there are only two ways out from here: going back the full distance you came, or weaving your body up through the irregular, vertical shaft you see here, affectionately called the birth canal."

With the memory of being born not immediately accessible to me as a point of reference, I foolishly chose the birth canal.

Any good therapist knows there are events in life so traumatic we stuff them deep into the subconscious. Still, images of darkness, feeling parts of my body pressed against other parts in a most unnatural way, and dangling stalactite-like midway into the canal have survived my will to suppress them.

And one other memory has survived: the voice of our guide calling out in the darkness, "Now raise your right hand over your head and grab the outcropping of rock just above you . . . now lift your right leg up and out as if stepping onto a small platform three feet away . . . turn your body to the sound of my voice . . . lay your chest on the ledge to your left and then pull your feet slowly up under you."

It never crossed my mind to question the guide's directives. I was in a desperate place. His voice was cool and confident. And, in time, I was born into light.

In time, we too are borne into light, into the understanding of God's perfect will. Meanwhile we sense for God, we listen for his voice, grateful that life's mysteries are only mysteries to us, not to God.

But still, we wrestle. We want to know what's happening to us and why it's happening. As one of my clients said at the beginning of her first session, "I don't even need to know where I'm going; I would consider counseling a great success if I could just get a handle on where I am."

Throughout this book I have been suggesting that the

modern church is losing its perspective on where it is and, consequently, on where it is going. And I have offered three guiding thoughts as to how its imaginative spirit might be reengaged. As we look more closely at the role of mystery in faith, I think this would be a good time to recall, and keep close at hand, those three templates:

- Regardless of how things might sometimes seem, God is with you here, now.
- Our industriousness is to flow from the bounty of our transformed hearts and wills, not the other way around.
- This transformation of the self occurs primarily within the context of our concrete, often challenging commitments.

Do you wrestle with understanding where God is and what he wants? Do you sometimes find his "blessings" to be rather peculiar . . . somewhat mysterious? You're not alone.

LIVING WITH MYSTERY

On Wrestling

The story in Genesis 32 of Jacob wrestling "the man" is a curious one. At first reading it seems an even match; as they struggle through the night, Jacob is unable to coerce from the man a blessing, and the man is unable to free himself from Jacob.

Who is this man? Why won't he just bless Jacob and be done with it?

Why do they wrestle in the dark, anyway? The simple take on it is that we, like Jacob, are to persist in our insistence that God bless us—that we are to desire God's blessing so much that we will refuse to let him go until it is ours. But I think there are some other lessons here as well.

As you may remember, to this point Jacob's life had been rather sordid. He had been manipulative and deceptive. He had not only tricked his dying father, Isaac, into giving him Esau's blessing, but later in his life he also craftily gleaned for himself the strong and healthy goats and sheep from his uncle Laban's flocks.

He had learned there is always a way to get what you want. And what he now wanted was his wrestling partner's blessing.

And blessing he eventually gets.

But here's the twist: In wrestling this man, two things happen to Jacob: (1) he is wounded, and (2) he realizes that he has met God face-to-face and hasn't died in the encounter. By the end of the story, it's as if the original blessing he fought so desperately for becomes an afterthought.

Initially seeking a blessing that would make his life better, he greets the light of day with a life transformed.

Genesis 32:30 tells us, "So Jacob called the place Peniel, saying, 'It is because I saw God face to face, and yet my life was spared.'" From this point forward, Jacob is a different sort of man. In place of conniving and arrogance we find greater patience and humility.

Much like Jacob, our own wrestling with God is not usually a five-minute match. True encounters with God aren't cheap and easy. They are life-changing. They expose the dark intentions of our lukewarm hearts and set us on a truer path, a path on which we sometimes go limping into our blessings.

Whenever we wrestle with God, we can always count on being transformed. In this, there is no mystery at all.

In the folder of one of my former clients is a touching, appreciative letter he sent to me about two years after I last sat with him. Although the receipt of such a letter is not that unusual, the circumstances surrounding my time with this particular client were.

Daniel was one of only two clients I have ever seen in my counseling practice whom I pleaded with God to never bring back. Of the twelve sessions we had together, the first ten were brutal. Daniel, a partner in a struggling law firm, had often refused to sit down (he said it gave me too much power), had slammed my door so hard it bent one of the hinge pins, had suggested that my lineage was something other than *Homo sapiens,* and had threatened no less than five times to sue me.

Determined to get him out of my office and out of my life, I called every referral source I could think of. But no one, mysteriously enough, had room for him in their practice. God had clearly made a mistake in sending him to me, and it was time for God to take him back. But God wouldn't cooperate. Like a bad dream, Daniel kept returning. And I kept wrestling with God.

The essence of the letter I keep handy in Daniel's folder is this: "Wayne, thanks for not giving up on me. Thanks for seeing in me a human being in need of help instead of a monster doing everything he could to alienate the people around him."

And then this: "Thanks for dragging me, screaming and kicking, back to my faith."

What Daniel doesn't know (even to this day) is that I initially *had* given up on him, that I nearly *did* see him as a monster, and that I had hoped he would be so offended by my spiritual proselytizing that he would leave.

It wasn't until we both went limping into sessions eleven and twelve that I finally saw why God had brought Daniel into my life. I saw that, for whatever healing I was bringing to Daniel's life, he was bringing something just as significant to mine.

In sticking with Daniel, God had changed *me*. In seeing the commitment through, I had come to a new appreciation of why people's stories must be fully told, how people's actions often smokescreen the more essential pain in their hearts, and what a critical role a listener can play in one's healing. All basic things, I know. But my time with Daniel was the transforming event that branded each of these things into the fabric of my future life and work.

Through Daniel, I had wrestled with God . . . he had won . . . and I had emerged a different person. And I learned that if we're not willing to wrestle—if we're not willing to suspend our native bent toward ease and safety— we won't see the surprises of transformation God works in our lives.

On Letting Go

There is wrestling, and then there is letting go. Another mystery of faith is why we must often release a thing in order to find it. One of the most difficult things a life of faith requires is letting go—whether it be relationship, material treasure, aspiration, or sacred cow. Letting go, however, must not be confused with giving up on or getting rid of as one would the residual clutter in one's house at a garage sale.

What I mean by letting go is resisting the impulse to control outcomes. To let go is to be open to a course of action or a way of thinking that might initially seem less secure.

In his provocative book *The Prophetic Imagination,* Walter Brueggemann suggests that the dominant culture (forged by society and largely adopted by the Christian community) is a numbing, unimaginative one. He suggests that it perpetuates a nearly unconscious "only now matters" form of living that has no informative history or future vision. "Our consumer culture," he says, "is organized against history. There is a depreciation of memory and a ridicule of hope, which means everything must be held in the now, either an urgent now or an eternal now. Either way, a community rooted in energizing memories and summoned by radical hopes is a curiosity and a threat in such a culture."[2]

I am similarly convinced that trust in the security of Christian principles is being confused with faith in God. Rather than engage a faith that requires, well, a little too much faith (not to mention the inherent wrestling), we find safe harbor in the surrogate stability of Right Christian Living. To allow God's uncontrollable ways to work their power in our lives is so much more refreshing and inspiring and, yes, less predictable. This is the way of faith, which is the very heart of the Christian's journey.

In the guise of good stewardship and sound thinking, our faith is fashioning for itself a well-oiled hamster wheel.

Though secure and productive (it spins well), the contraption leaves little to the imagination. Granted, for the harried traveler nothing is more calming than the hum of a spinning wheel. But nothing is more numbing.

On my desk is a flyer for a nearby church's Wednesday evening classes. "Tired of ineffective prayer?" it asks. "Join us this Wednesday evening and get your prayers answered!"

Yes, it is good to pray. But it is also good to trust and to wait and to sometimes not get what we pray for.

I have found myself apologizing to new clients before I even begin counseling them. Aware that people visit therapists for solutions to problems—that is, solutions for how to add or restore something they don't have or have lost (peace of mind, fulfilling relationships, a sense of who they are)—I feel compelled to warn them that there is a good chance I will, instead, be helping them let go of something.

It's a difficult sell, because many see letting go as losing rather than gaining. For many, images of exploding space shuttles, drug-injected teenagers, heart attacks, and highway calamities enforce the notion that if you don't control it (whatever "it" may be), it will get the best of you. It will ambush you, pull you under with its massive, hydraulic jaws, leap on you from the treetops like a gang of rabid howler monkeys.

To let go is to lose control, to be eaten alive, and *that* is not acceptable.

But let me state it clearly: the impulse to control—to get it all lined up—is often a manifestation of fear, not faith.

We might pump up the principles and send them floating overhead like the Goodyear blimp with the words *Right Christian Living* branded bold and tall on its shimmering skin. But the fiery sparks of real life always bring it back to earth, sometimes in a nose dive, Hindenburg fashion. The beguiled Christians falling from the spiritual dirigible as it tilts, groans, and bursts into flames, often land on my couch. "Why didn't it work?" they ask. "Right Christian Living was supposed to keep me aloft . . . freed from my childhood hurt, rising above my bent toward sin, successful in my marriage and employment." I usually wait a few sessions before suggesting that perhaps the ship's pilot was someone other than God.

It didn't work, I then tell them, because principles— Christian or not—will always fail you. At some point, your "decency" will spring a leak; your "good parenting" will buckle under the weight of human frailty; the shocking crack in your "best intentions" will reveal a darker motive. You have been looking to these things to save you, not guide you, I say. Sometimes they understand this, and sometimes they don't. And sometimes they ask for a book on how to get the blimp up and running again.

Whether big church, small church, friend, foe, seminar,

convention, or small-group Bible study—if the dominant message you hear is that the application of "biblical principles" to your past, your future, your loved ones, your faith will automatically set you free . . . then flee at once! Far better to cast your lot with those who see the wisdom in letting go.

I'm not saying don't immerse yourself in the Bible. Do so, but not in order to dissect it for principles; rather, soak in its stories, ache in its anguish and sing in its joys, find life in its truth about God's love for mankind, be shaped by its character-forming wisdom.

In Christ there is certainly rest for the weary. But the rest we ultimately find is in direct proportion to what we are able to release, not conquer. Learning to let go is life's greater spiritual challenge.

Years ago I took a water safety course. The instructor was showing us how to rescue someone who was in trouble in the water. "Swimming them to safety is the easiest part of the rescue," he said. "Getting them to stop struggling—to trust you and relax a little—that's the hard part."

God's mysteries are there to set us free, to lift from our backs the weight of having to make it all work. God has no interest in showing us how to resolve life's mysteries. He is the how. He is the Living Water. It is he himself we are drawn to in the midst of our crumbling Christian principles.

We are to love our God, wrestle, celebrate, and labor over that which we are given stewardship—and then stand with the angels in eternal perspective, marveling at how God knows each mystery's plot before it even begins.

chapter 6

SEEING FRAGMENTATION

> The house of God is not a safe place. It is
> a cross where time and eternity meet,
> and where we are — or should be —
> challenged to live more vulnerably,
> more interdependently.
> MADELEINE L'ENGLE, *Glimpses of Grace*

Whatever apocalyptic stories you may have heard about rotator-cuff operations, don't believe them . . . the real thing is much worse!

The rotator cuff is basically that place in your shoulder where the upper arm's ball meets the shoulder's socket. This cuff is tethered bone-to-bone by a major tendon enabling the arm to flap itself up and down. In my case, the left rotator-cuff tendon had become about 80 percent torn, making it impossible to lift my arm more than thirty or forty degrees from my side. I could shake your hand, no problem. But lifting it through the car window to grab my parking validation from the ticker required the assistance of my right arm and hand, and spurred a predictable stab of pain.

I kept thinking it would just get better on its own. After a year or so of such compensatory antics and a few involuntary, Tourettes-like expressions of agony, I decided it wouldn't.

Two weeks after surgery I sat half propped up on my right side and half asleep in my study's leather chair, praying for Armageddon, when suddenly—horror of horrors—the arm started slipping. I had earlier loosened the sling for comfort, trusting the useless arm would drape over my left side like one of those lazy lions on a tree limb. Instead—and in slow motion—I found myself in a race against time. Hoping to snag my left arm before it fell to my back, I simultaneously rolled to my left and thrust my right hand out across my chest. I lost the race. All I snagged was thin air.

Now, lie on your right side and let your left arm drop behind you. No big deal, right? But then have your trusted (but very twisted) friend press slivers of broken glass into your shoulder as it falls. An exaggeration, you say? Just ask any rotator-cuff vet. With the exception of my sixth-grade flu shot debacle, this was the only time in my life I remember momentarily losing consciousness because of pain.

As my left arm slipped from its perch, I think I would

have given my right arm for some stabilizing tension. But an arm such as mine, connected to nothing but gravity, had no way of saving itself. It could do nothing but fall. Separated from the rest of the body, it was rendered useless.

In the aliveness of pain, I discovered in this incident an important lesson: the necessity of all the parts of the body of Christ for each other. An indispensable trait of our faith is its capacity to hold each part in tension. This tension, this interdependence, is critical to faith's strength and to the health of the body of Christ.

For it is within this tension that the Christian faith finds its vibrancy. Yet it is this very same tension we seem compelled to destroy. It's as though the body of Christ would rather have its arms, legs, feet, and hands atrophy than have them strengthened in the tug, let's say, between evangelical and charismatic, pre-trib and post-trib, conservative and liberal, Southern Baptist and Anglican.

Though perhaps well intended—out of concern that we need to make certain the Christ we worship is the Christ of the Bible—this penchant for compartmentalizing the disparate voices of faith is mostly unhelpful. It is a way of keeping us as far away from each other as possible, a way of isolating—and thus separating—our body's parts.

In place of separating ourselves from each other, I propose a simple test: Does your heart know Christ? Do your eyes see his face and your voice cry out, "My Lord and my God"? And do your hands and feet then feed the poor, give water to the thirsty, walk the extra mile? In other words, are you converted to Christ? Are you converted in such a way that not even your pet theological distinctions can hold a candle to the joy of knowing Christ and sharing in his life with the rest of his rag-tag followers?

Yes?

Then I don't care how uncomfortable you make me, or anyone else. I don't care how unlike me you are. If it is Christ that binds us bone-to-bone and spirit-to-spirit, then that is enough. I welcome the tension on your end of the spiritual tendon. It helps lift our body's ailing arms toward heaven.

OF FRAGMENTS AND FRACTURES

Spiritual Reductionism

God's great goal, as the apostle Paul outlines it, is to gather his people into one magnificent structure, a dwelling place for God:

> *You are no longer foreigners and aliens, but fellow*
> *citizens with God's people and members of God's*
> *household, built on the foundation of the apostles*
> *and prophets, with Christ Jesus himself as the chief*

cornerstone. In him the whole building is joined together and rises to become a holy temple in the Lord. And in him you too are being built together to become a dwelling in which God lives by his Spirit. (EPHESIANS 2:19-22)

Amazing! What a cascade of images of welcoming and gathering and building and joining and dwelling together. But in this great construction project—here in this initial redeemed/yet-still-being-redeemed, holy/yet-still-unholy state—two things happen that make for a surprising spiritual dynamic: we get very resistant, and God gets very creative.

As the author of creativity, God must enjoy the unorthodox humor of pairing a stern father with a feisty, independent son or daughter; a passive husband with an aggressive wife; a collegiate environmentalist with a future oilman roommate. I think he enjoys the relationships that exist between the apparently incompatible. Our trials and temptations, our head-butting relationships and disagreements are not the intruders they seem. God sees them as the transforming spice of the spiritual life.

I recently saw an advertisement for a Christian book by an author claiming that the foundation of any successful romantic relationship was the degree to which the couple could think and act alike. The book's ad even offered a checklist that would solve the dilemma of whether a romance should continue or not. Just score 90 percent and you're in! Anything less and (I assume) you are out of God's will and deserve whatever romantic calamities might befall you.

I've long puzzled over God's will regarding the mysteries of human compatibility, so I should be relieved now to have access to the details of The Romantic Master Plan. The checklist should be just the ticket for my love-struck, starry-eyed clients. Having reduced the mystery of romance to a questionnaire, I'm sure they will now be able to avoid any future tension in their relationship.

Poet and essayist Wendell Berry writes, "The principle that is opposite to reduction — and, when necessary, its sufficient answer — is God's love for all things, for each thing for its own sake and not for its category."[1] If we seek just enough perspective to resist dismissing Berry's statement as a kind of frothy "all is one and one is all" elixir, we see that he has it right. "For everything God created is good," said Paul in 1 Timothy 4:4. "And nothing is to be rejected." And I believe the traces of this goodness are best understood in their plurality, in the encounter *between* our faith's various voices, not in their exclusive entombing.

Righteous Wrongness

In *The Screwtape Letters,* C. S. Lewis exposes for us one of Satan's masterful tricks. He shows us how Satan assuages his own angst over our becoming Christians by engaging his backup plan: rendering us ineffective. When Satan is able to isolate us from each other and distract us from the essential truth that God is with us, he's one happy devil. And I think one of the most effective ways Satan does this dividing and conquering is to pare the various elements of the Christian experience—at both personal and community levels—into impotent, warring fragments.

What are the attitudes that serve to divide us? There's so much we could say—and so many have done so—about how human beings need to quit fighting with one another. But instead of a "Can't we all just get along?" kind of approach, I think a more productive process is to look at our root attitudes toward God. How do we use our faith to put us in competition with God and depersonalize him (and in so doing, depersonalize our spouses, family members, coworkers, strangers)? Here are some fragmenting attitudes I've identified.

The so-that faith—"I will serve God, be a good Christian, so that . . . " So that God will bless me, things will go well, I will find relief from my struggles, my children will turn out well.

Here's the fragmenting result of so-that faith: When I set out to earn God's favor, I subtly distance myself from him. He becomes someone to conjure, to manipulate. He becomes *something* out there I act *at* rather than *someone* close to me

I act *with*. This depersonalizes him. He becomes an it rather than a he, and no love can pass between us.

Concurrently, so-that faith depersonalizes other people. All my efforts to win God's favor come crashing to the ground when I look over the fence and see that my neighbor has life better than me. I make comparisons through eyes blind with jealousy. Jealousy and envy become the undercurrents of my thought life: "How could so-and-so be more blessed than I am when she has done so little to deserve it?" I gloat when disaster strikes next door: "Well, he was so proud. He had it coming. Perhaps he'll learn a little humility."

Of the many Christians visiting my office, a disproportionate number are "so-that" disciples. But what's so amazing is that even when the so-that train has come barreling brakeless through the thin-walled terminal of the Right Christian Living station, the bargaining for blessings continues. "Help me see what I did wrong," they plead, "so that I'll be back in God's favor . . . so that I can enjoy the good life."

But there is such a fundamental difference between the good life and the abundant one. Such a difference between wanting God and wanting what God can give us. The New Testament model is that we desire God *because* his love has captured us, enthralled us. Consequently, the primary protection we enjoy is not protection from the fray of life, but the protection of our souls. It is first and foremost in God's love, not in his blessings, that we find sanctuary. "The body they may kill [it may all be turned upside down and inside out]; God's truth abideth still."[2] This truest of all loves—not the resolution of my difficult circumstances—is what carries me forth.

The appeasing faith—Appeasing faith is a distinct twist on so-that faith in that it tries less to coerce a blessing from God than to stay God's hand. The appeasing faith has rightly determined that God is a jealous and wrathful and uncompromising God. And who of us would not desire to calm a raging bull, especially if we knew we would be spending our earthly (not to mention eternal) life in the bull's arena?

But the story is only half told. God is jealous of that which devours our misspent affections. He is wrathful toward what is arrogantly unjust. He is uncompromising in the severe purity of his love. To yield his jealousy, his wrath, his strong-headedness would be to stop loving us. And the god remaining would be no god at all.

Any effort of ours to appease God is doomed from the start. Only the sinless Christ, who drank the cup of God's wrath on the cross for us, has satisfied, has completely exhausted, God's wrath. And we can only come to him empty-handed as grateful beneficiaries.

The "virtuous partnership" faith—The virtuously faithful Christian takes great comfort in being a good person, discerning and practicing proper religious etiquette, being a good, respectable team player. "Let's go shake out the kinks," a seminary friend was fond of saying when we were workout bound. If not thoughtfully considered, the virtuous Christian life too easily becomes an exercise in practicing religion—of keeping honed our spiritual dexterity, shaking out the Christian kinks.

The virtuous Christian life is really moralism. It often doesn't admit to sin, because sins are things that murderers, thieves, and adulterers do. It ignores the deep undercurrents of jealousy, anger, vengefulness, and lust. It is empty of true contrition and repentance. It doesn't seek to intimately know the God of Isaiah: "I live in a high and holy place, but also with him who is contrite and lowly in spirit, to revive the spirit of the lowly and to revive the heart of the contrite."[3]

The virtuous Christian participates in a kind of fraternal *quid pro quo*. "Tradies," says my wife when she wants a back rub. You rub my back and I'll rub yours. Much like returning a favor to a neighbor because he helped build our fence, we serve God because it's the proper, decent, virtuous response. "Me and my buddy, God, are partners in making this a better world," says the virtuous Christian.

Recognize this particular approach to faith? It's a breeding ground for judgmentalism. Where "virtuous partnership" and "so-that" theologies are coupled, there is little patience or room left for horse-and-buggy faith.

The power faith—I think of power faith as an angry version of virtuous partnership. "Me and my buddy, God, are partners in making this a better world, darn it! So get big, or go home!" When Right Christian Living drifts into right Christian loathing, someone—either within the church or without—needs to be held accountable. It's those liberals! Those conservatives! Those Americans! Those Middle Easterners! Those gays . . . those feminists . . . those Pentecostals . . .

In Berkeley Breathed's irresistible, short, animated film, *A Wish for Wings That Work,* we find Opus (a frustrated penguin) writing Santa, lobbying him for wings. In the letter's opening he states, "As your record should show, I'm a bird . . . specifically, a penguin; an accident of birth for which I do not blame my mother. I prefer to blame . . . (long pause) . . . Congress."[4]

That's it! It's got to be Congress! They're the ones messing it all up!

Thank God for the power he has entrusted to us Christians, say the powerful faithful. Thank God for the power (and the attendant right) to string *them* up by their toes. To demean, shame, and hold *them all* accountable for their ungodly theology and despicable lives.

It's all going to the dogs and someone needs to take the fall.

Maybe Opus is right. Maybe the real problem is Congress.

Do you recognize any of these fragmenting attitudes? At worst, each attitude insists that it has figured God out. The truly passionate faith, on the other hand, recalls God's own patience and grace as a pattern for our relating with one another. Understanding and applying the implications of this patience and grace is the Christian's most basic work.

An Urgent but Loving Call

When those who know little of the Christian faith look on this band of Christ-ones, do they see a people who are able to tug and pull and strengthen one another through discourse and genuine concern for the other's well-being? Or do they see a spiritual version of the cliquish high school cafeteria?

By keeping us separated, Satan renders us ineffective. He knows that as long as he can keep our fragmented *doing* from penetrating the fullness of our *being,* then the transforming work of the Spirit can be held at bay.

In Ephesians 4, the apostle Paul sounds an urgent but loving call:

> *Be completely humble and gentle; be patient, bear-*
> *ing with one another in love. Make every effort to*
> *keep the unity of the Spirit through the bond of*

*peace. . . . Speaking the truth in love, we will in all
things grow up into him who is the Head, that is,
Christ. From him the whole body, joined and held
together by every supporting ligament, grows and
builds itself up in love, as each part does its work.
(verses 2-3, 15-16)*

These are the words of an imaginative faith. Each part
of the body is crucial. None is dispensable. And all the parts
are held together by love. Paul wants more than anything
for us to grasp the love of Christ. Why? Because he knows
if we can taste even a hint of this love, our life of faith and
our fellowship with the rest of the body of Christ will be
filled with the fullness and the wholeness of God himself.

chapter 7

SEEING WHOLENESS

"I wish I could go all the way with you to
Rivendell, Mr. Frodo, and see Mr. Bilbo," said Sam.
"And yet the only place I really want to be in is
here. I am that torn in two."
"Poor Sam. . . . It will feel like that, I am afraid,"
said Frodo, "But you will be healed —
you were meant to be
solid and whole, and you will be."
J. R. R. TOLKIEN, *The Return of the King*

---

ith one hand tightly gripping the hayloft's splintered door frame, a young boy with tousled hair and sunburned face leaned his eager torso as far out of the opening as he could without falling. On the western horizon a shock of brilliant red sky and a churning plume of dust chased a Model T Ford along the dry country road toward the barn. "Here comes Cliff!" the boy shouted.

"The fiddler's coming!"

By sunset, lanterns were aglow and barn mice scurried about as the fiddler pulled his strong, calloused fingers along the strings and neck of his beloved instrument—a rare and cherished treasure he had found nestled among a tin peddler's more practical wares. With the final, frenetic chorus of "Roll Out the Barrel" still hanging in the air, Cliff snatched his hat from his beaded brow, mocked a regal bow to the grateful dancers, and let loose a robust, infectious laugh. On this bountiful, hard-worked farmland on the plains of eastern Colorado, no one was more respected, more loved, and more trusted than Cliff. Though tattered and chastened by the farm's harsh demands, he loved his life. He loved his family, his friends, his God. Cliff was one of the passionate ones. Clifford Allen was my grandfather.

We all know a Cliff. Each of us can recall those people who infect us with a quality that seems to defy labeling. "What is it about these people?" we find ourselves asking. "Why do I want nothing more than just to be where they are?"

It's not their power. Not their status. Not their achievements. These things are far too pretentious. I think we crave their company because they are present and real. Whether gentle, firm, pensive, practical, or playful, these people infuse all they encounter—like a fine perfume—with a passionate aura, with a sense that they are fully alive.

I believe we are magnetically drawn to the truly passionate ones because—though not godlike—they are most like God. They best reflect God's creative complexities. His knowledge beyond words. His impassioned love. Yes, even his pain.

We have a sense that even in their imperfection, they are whole.

But if wholeness is not perfection, then what is it? Is the juxtaposition of partial yet whole, imperfect yet holy, broken yet complete, nothing more than a clever word-joust, or is there hidden within these seeming opposites a spiritual paradox?

IMPERFECTLY WHOLE

The following dialogue with one of my clients took place about four hours ago. Before I give it to you as verbatim as I can, you'll need to know that Jan is not the client's real name and that her boss and I are acquainted. The conversation picks up with Jan telling me her boss is now aware that after fifteen years with the company, Jan will be leaving.

Jan: Well, the cat's out of the bag.

WB: You alluded to that in your phone message.

Jan: Yeah . . . when I told my boss I wasn't going to accept the incentive package they were offering in exchange for another three-year commitment, he knew something was up. I told him I needed a break—a big one. He said, What do you mean? I said I was going to leave the company after I closed the deal I was working on.

WB: What happened then?

Jan: He was shocked. He asked me what Wayne thought about this. I told him you supported my decision.

WB: Thanks a lot, Jan. There goes my only referral source.

Jan: (laughs) He said, I want you to ask Wayne if he has any idea how much money you make.

WB: Well, tell him I don't know and I don't want to know. Tell him that it's one thing to make a living but quite another to make a life. Tell him I said that Jan doesn't need more money . . . she needs a life . . . and that she'll suffocate without it.

Jan: Isn't that the truth! My boss doesn't get it. He thinks I'm having a midlife crisis.

WB: I think I'd call it a no-life crisis.

Jan is right—her boss doesn't get it. Her boss thinks that nothing could possibly be more important than increasing one's net worth. Somewhere out there in the midst of "finally, enough money to be happy" is the blissful life. I happen to know that Jan's boss is miserable. But I'm sure his misery isn't permanent; it will end as soon as he gets "just enough money to be happy."

Now, be honest. In our theology, aren't we more often like Jan's boss than like Jan? Somewhere out there is a cache of spiritual wealth, we reason. Just one more link in the chain and it will all come together. Just one more *really* fervent prayer, one more spiritual insight, one more Wednesday evening Bible course. What a glorious day that will be when we finally reap the rewards—the long life, the healthy body, the exceptional children, marriage, and lifestyle—that were to come with our commitment to Christ.

As I have suggested many times throughout this book, the culprit is never the prayers, the insights, the Bible studies, the conventions themselves, but the ways in which we employ these spiritual tools to help us gain God's blessings rather than God. The danger is that we greatly cheapen the rich spiritual life God has for us when we distill it into spiritual sound bytes, when we bottle it and label it like a tonic, a balm for our spiritual gout.

There was a time when I read the passage "be perfect as God is perfect" as "be perfect *because* God is perfect." Be perfect because you will otherwise be imperfect. He is perfect; you are not. Big trouble—right here in River City! Get busy, you have a long way to go!

Thankfully, that time has long passed. I now read this passage the way it was written: be perfect *as* God is perfect.

That is, be perfect in the same way.

So in what way is God perfect?

He wildly creates. He takes his Sabbath meal from a grain field, holds up children as the model of what the kingdom of God is like, wears a nasty, purple scar on his side. He despises injustice and is heavy-handed with those who defile what is holy. He is gentle, forgiving, and has been known to cry at the tomb of a loved one or even a city he cares deeply about. In nature and in prayer he finds solace and communion with his own being. He is both man of sorrow and author of the greatest joys known. He inhabits atoms, galaxies, and the complex emotions of the human heart. He is past, present, and future; he is justice and peace; he is love incarnate.

Now *that's* perfection. Because God himself—not our will to *be* something—is our true center, this perfection breathes. It feels the thorns imbedded in its brow, has dust on its feet, knows the anguish of a broken heart.

Near the end of Tolkien's *The Return of the King,* the Days of the Rings having passed, we find Sam, Frodo, Bilbo, and some of the elves and other companions riding by horseback to the shore of the sea for Bilbo and Frodo's send-off. Tolkien lets us in on their state of mind: "With them went many Elves of the High Kindred who would no longer stay in Middle-earth; and among them, *filled with a sadness that was yet blessed and without bitterness,* rode Sam, and Frodo, and Bilbo, and the Elves delighted to honor them."[1]

Whatever wholeness we find on this earth will have a similar bent to it. It will be seasoned with a sadness that is nevertheless blessed and without bitterness. Rather than being an achieved perfection, this kind of wholeness is more a redeemed imperfection. Although the distinction may seem to some insignificant, those who know the weight of this purposeful sadness also know its substantiality, its eternal qualities.

In chapter 3 I stated that living in the present doesn't mean living for the moment, but rather, bringing to this moment an eternal perspective. Similarly, when I seek *God with me now*—within the mix of my sadness, woundedness, and joy—I am as close to being as whole as I can be on this earth. In the endless present, I welcome to my imperfections not only the perspective and wisdom of a perfect God, but also God himself.

In this way, in a single breath, the Clifford Allens of this world can say, "I am wounded and imperfect" and "my life is whole." And we know they are telling the truth.

When it was clear to my father after his sudden heart attack that he had just hours left to live, and as I sat at his bedside stroking his clammy brow, he said to me, "Son, either way, I win. If I live, I get to have more time with my family, and if I die, I go to be with God." Either way, Dad felt his life would be whole because his God was at the center of each possibility.

I wish my seminary had offered a course on spiritual CPR. I am daily tending in my counseling practice the wounds of shell-shocked Christians. They are exhausted with trying to do all the right things; dizzy with confusion about their difficult lives; choking on the disingenuous smiles and platitudes of some of their fellow Christians.

But it would be shortsighted to dismiss their angst as the manifestation of a lack of faith. Although they have, on the one hand, deep appreciation and a degree of sophistication concerning the core truths of their lives in Christ, they also know that the directions are missing a page. Somewhere between "he gave his life to Christ" and "he lived happily ever after" are the operating instructions on what to do with *life*.

And I can't fault the instinct to fill in the "what do I do with life" gap with tricks of the Christian trade. But here is what I am lobbying for: At some point we need to realize that the personal security and keys to spiritual growth we seek will not be found in spiritual busyness or attainment. At some point we need to grab hold and live the life we have.

The great paradox is that our lives are most authentically spiritual when they are the least spiritualized. We are closest to Christ's breast when we eat, suffer, play, feel, mourn, rejoice, and yearn with him.

For many of us, our lives lack this intentionality. They are not fresh and responsive. Pinned to the grill of our eighteen wheeler faith, our view of the passing spiritual landscape is more subliminal than concrete. We are pulled along like dry leaves in a gusty breeze.

So what gives? How is it that some of us work so hard and yet flounder at faith's complexities, while others of us seem to have a sense of its pulse? I think the answer can be found in our view of wholeness.

ESSENTIALLY WHOLE

Realizing that I have already stated our premise in a variety of ways, I'll risk redundancy by stating it yet one more way: To find wholeness, seek and attend to the essence of what is already before you in your life, because that is where you will find your joy. "Rejoice before him," says David in words that deserve long and prayerful meditation in the context of *this* day's crisis, worry, puzzle, or peace (Psalm 68:4). Seek and live every thought and act as grounded in God's love. Let no second-best thing such as "being a good Christian" distract you from walking fully alert on the paths of transformation God has set before you in the real stuff of your life, in the commitments you have already made.

Live an exemplary life, certainly, but always with the perspective in mind that spiritual adeptness is not the ultimate goal of your faith. Your identity is in Christ—not in how well you have mastered someone else's idea of Right Christian Living.

The resolve to train our ears on Christ's voice and our eyes on his face demands of us a kind of imaginative spirit that is alien to our contemporary Christian practice. While it is not all that difficult to imagine what the Christian life in its most pristine state would look like, it is no minor challenge to see God's presence in this one that is so fractured and scattered.

A mechanically minded man I know told me of a television show he likes to watch. As he describes it, in this show a team of engineers is led to a large workshop strewn with pieces of sheet metal, iron rods, wheels, wires, and other basic junkyard parts. They are then told they have five hours to create from the tangled debris a fully operational lawn mower (for example).

As sparks fly and rivets flatten, a machine emerges that— although it is no Toro—will adequately sheer your lawn's green locks in time for the weekend cookout. Where I would look in the workshop and see nothing but a mess of metal, an engineer sees a lawn mower.

This is the kind of imagination a passionate faith employs. It sees not just wholeness, but a wholeness that breaks new ground in beauty and function. A wholeness that exceeds what anyone would have imagined possible, given the debris from which it is crafted.

With this in mind, and in closing this four-chapter section on the eyes of faith, here are a few thoughts on ways in which the imaginative Christian might conceptualize the essentials of an "imperfectly whole" life.

From Appearance to Essence

Casting off religion; putting on Christ—In the early years of my faith, while shifting my focus from a general spiritual life to one more specifically Christian, I would sometimes feel that I was part of a covert operation. I was infiltrating the unfamiliar realm of Christian fellowship, seeking classified information regarding the inner workings of the Christian life.

These were fertile years. Years in which my home church planted and watered many seeds.

Exposure to the wisdom and passion of guest preachers and speakers from Oxford and Scotland, from the best pulpits of California, New York, and Mississippi, from the most dynamic parachurch and world relief organizations, and from the immediate church community and staff was the baker's-dozen benefit of my church's commitment to growing its congregation into the image of Christ. I drank it in like a sponge. First Presbyterian Church of Colorado Springs set a standard by which I measure—even now, years after my involvement there—the vision of other ministries.

Even so, I think I started making the same mistake as the freed Israelites. I came to believe I was entitled to this feeding. I got fat on expectation. I was getting the hang of this Christianity thing, and it felt good.

And that was precisely the problem. I loved how Christianity *worked* and *looked*. It was such a dynamic means to a wonderful life.

As Christ's call to bear my cross and identify with him in his suffering began to get in the way of my "victorious" faith, I not only started replacing Christ/Lord of my life with Christ/CEO of the Society for Right Christian Living, but also decided I needed a powerful buffer to stave off any threat to my spiritual advancements. I joined a charismatic group and was baptized in the Holy Spirit. I spoke in tongues and led Bible studies. I also updated my infant baptism with a conversion-baptism for good measure.

I wince as I write this. It is so clear to me now how, in all of my religious maneuvering, I was trying to appropriate any weapon I could find—even the Holy Spirit himself—to defend myself against being transformed into the image of Christ.

This may all sound so blasphemous. And, for me at least, that is exactly what it was. I was a modern-day Pharisee, secretly proud I was not one of the spiritually unfortunate "others" who didn't understand how the spiritual life worked.

I remember in college reading Søren Kierkegaard's *Fear and Trembling* and being struck by his boldness at criticizing the arrogant spirituality of his generation. "Unless I am very much mistaken," he wrote, "this generation is rather inclined to be proud of making what they do not even believe I am capable of making, namely, incomplete movements (of faith)."[2] I was rather proud of the spiritual structure I had crafted. And I could neither hear Christ's voice nor see his face for the numbing arrogance of my industriousness.

You may have noticed in this book a certain lack of familiar Christian phraseology. This has been intentional. For many years now I have felt that my receptivity to Christ's voice depends somewhat on my willingness to hear Christ in whatever way he speaks. One of my first spiritually disrobing ah-hahs, in fact, was when I realized that Christ didn't speak evangelicalese, Lutheranese, Presbyterianese, Baptistinese, or fundamentalese. He speaks the truth in love. And in my life, at least, that truth was getting lost in the appearances of my faith.

Up-sized Christianity—In addition to casting off religion and putting on Christ, I believe another way we as a community of faith can return to some of faith's essentials is to resist the tug of equating size with success. Neither more, nor less, is more. Both big and small are overrated.

I sometimes think that we as Christians are the greatest perpetrators of the "size matters" madness that has settled into the marrow of our culture's bones. This wouldn't bother me if I believed that Christianity saw the relative size of its churches and programs as neutral. If I could believe that our large campuses and Christian organizations are not viewing their size as validation that they've got a more direct pipeline to God's blessings than those who struggle to stay afloat, then I would be far less prone to skepticism.

Conversely, if I could believe that the intention of some small fellowships was to grow people in Christ instead of growing the sometimes intolerable egos of their leaders, then perhaps I could get more enthusiastically on board.

If we in the Christian church could embrace the idea that size is neutral, how refreshingly uncluttered would be the message being preached from the pulpit . . . or in the books . . . or at the conferences . . . or from the tube. The "professional" Christian survival pattern, however, appears to be little different from the secular one. As one giant bill-board in Colorado Springs proclaims, "Jesus Saves, Jesus Heals, Jesus Satisfies." And we can up-size that for you, if you'd like.

In a size-matters Christianity there is no room for com-mercial *or spiritual* "failure." There is no room left for God's way *not* being our way. *Of course* God wants big and impressive. *Of course* God wants small and intimate. *Of course* God wants it the way *we* want it.

To suggest that the commercial success of a Christian fellowship, program, or product is God's stamp of approval of that endeavor is to be deceived by a shallow wealth. It is the modern version of the camel.

Pray to God that his grace will widen the needle's eye!

From Gold to Stone

What if we believed the journey of faith was actually more of an awakening to what we already have than a striving after what we think will complete us?

What if we individually, and as a body, stopped for just a moment and asked these questions: Is it just possible that God's sustenance can be found right here within this life I am currently living? Is it just possible that the seed of my wholeness has already been planted in these commitments I've made?

From the perspective I have as a counselor, it is clear to me that the new is almost always more enticing than the transformed. We would rather start over with something new and fresh than face the transformation required to complete what we've already begun.

Who of us hasn't longed—sometimes desperately so— for a new venue? Who of us hasn't desired to just slip away from the difficult marriage, the demanding children, the responsibilities of caring for fragile elders, the burden of a ravaged childhood? Understandably, we often feel that we would rather take our chances with a fresh start than face the healing fires of our transformation.

As much as we don't want to admit it, the modern Christian culture perpetuates the lottery myth. We talk about the Christian life as we would about becoming a billionaire. Wouldn't it be nice if . . . I wonder what it would take to . . . If I could just get this one thing in place, then . . .

We encourage one another to escape into the dreaminess of the life we don't have. In this we miss the one we're in.

Yes, we might find initial relief in our escape, but we won't find the liberation that comes with being changed. The crosses of our lives must bear their full weight before their glory can be revealed. And this glory—this wholeness of perspective and character—is found most authentically and paradoxically within the imperfection of our most common commitments.

In thinking we can find wholeness in anything other than our transformation, we trade the Living Water of Christ himself for the cosmetic appeal of a golden god.

Let's not make that mistake. Let's help each other see Christ in the lives we live.

Part Three

THE TRANSFORMED LIFE

chapter 8

HOW SELF IS TRANSFORMED

The horrors of Ravensbruck, especially Betsie's
death, caused me to wake up to reality. When
I did, I was able to see that when all the securities
of the world are falling away, then you realize,
like never before, what it means to have
your security in Jesus.
CORRIE TEN BOOM, *Prison Letters*

———————— ≈ ————————

To this point I have been painting a portrait of a
truer way of faith. Not truer in the sense of being
more Christian, but truer in the sense of being freer of spiritual consumerism. More on the mark in its capacity to discern the cosmetic elements of the Christian life from the
more essential.

In reminding us that God is with us here and now, that
God is most interested in our transformation not our

industriousness, and that this transformation is engaged most directly in the commitments and relationships we daily encounter, I have been steering us toward a more journey-based faith.

With this in mind, I would now like to shift gears just a bit and consider in these final three chapters how all of this translates into the lives we wake up to.

Let's begin in a very private place.

PRIVATE PLACES

Preparing a Table for Two

When the waiter approached and asked Beth and me where we wanted to sit, I was quick to say, "The most private table you have." It was a special night. I had just asked Beth to marry me, and she had said yes. I had even by phone wrangled from her father and mother a blessing of my intentions. Given Beth's rebellious childhood and very independent character, I think they were relieved she wouldn't be marrying a Sandinista rebel or an alien mutant. I would do just fine. They were happy to have me onboard.

Beth and I were engaging a decision of grand proportion, and so we sat in a cozy, private little corner of the restaurant collecting our thoughts and hearts.

To a degree, time with God is similar. When alone with

God, we stem the buzz of life just long enough to gather our thoughts—to pay attention to why we're buzzing at all. As we bring our pulse rates down a notch or two, we discover that most of our buzzing is just that—noise. The noise! The self-talk, the high-speed rattle of modern technology, the brain clutter. It numbs and mesmerizes us to a point that it is nearly impossible to hear the sound that matters most: the sound of God's heart beating in concert with our own.

As I see it, the point of this set-aside time is to attend more consciously to Who has been there all along. When I am alone with God in this way, I look into his heart, not his wallet. Instead of seeking hits of spiritual adrenaline, I am seeking the face of the one who sustains me, regardless.

But even our most private times with God are so saturated with distractions and counterproductive imperatives that we have little sense of his nearness. Too often we approach time with God as just that: a *time* slotted between soccer practice and the evening meal, between the morning business meeting and noon workout.

Although we might not believe it theologically, the Christianity we actually practice is one in which God is not always nearby. He is only near when we have cleaned up our lives enough to have him over for a quick bite or when something has gone wrong and we need him to guide and, hopefully, rescue us.

For the passionate Christian, the contrasting thought is a very simple one: God is with me. Always. I do not need to conjure, cajole, entice, woo, or find him. I need to embrace him, to converse with him about what my life is and what it isn't, and to recognize his incomparable wisdom and glory. I need to lift the refreshing and sustaining cup of Living Water that he is to my spiritual lips, and drink him in.

In my alone time with God—just as in my life in general—I am first and foremost to be cognizant of the One sitting with me. I am to remember that he is already present, that he is already powerful, and that he already loves me. Rather than seek ways to get the faucet flowing or the power booted up, I seek the spiritual eyes to see what is directly in front of me.

Looking across the table of faith into the face of the God who loves me and knows me intimately, I begin the transformational journey with the simplest of prayers: *Lord, help me see what I already have.*

Preparing for Transformation

So, what can we expect when we open ourselves to God in this way? What can we expect of the transformational process—not only in these private moments with God, but in our spiritual journey in general? In our time with family?

In our time with the community at large? What, exactly, is God wanting us to see?

First, he is wanting us to see that he, alone, is our hope.

Second, he is wanting us to see truth. He is wanting us to see what is directly in front of us. And there is no way to encounter the truth about our lives without encountering pain.

Third, he is wanting us to wait. He is wanting our thoughts and desires to complete their journey into the core of our soulful being, where they cannot be distracted by our insidiously powerful fears, angers, and insecurities. He is wanting our desire for results and answers to be made subject to the rich but sometimes uncompromisingly slow pace of our spiritual transformation.

Finally, in this waiting he is wanting us to bask so fully in his presence that we begin to see our life through his eyes, to stand so confidently and unpretentiously at his side that we are able to see what he sees. It is only in this way—in this miraculous unfolding of God's fiery, passionate transformation of our being—that we are set free to love God, ourselves, and others. In preparing to be transformed, then, we are ultimately preparing to know the freedom that is already ours in Christ.

As severe as it is, transformation is nevertheless a great gift—one that must be unpacked to be understood. So let's now consider briefly how the transformational process moves from hope, to truth, to patience, to sight, and—finally—to the fruit of the process, which is love's freedom.

THE GIFTS OF TRANSFORMATION

On our engagement day, I gave Beth the gift of a ring, my love, and ultimately, a life together on this earth. God's transformational gifts, however, are not so neatly packaged. They are bought with Christ's blood, bound with a crown of thorns, secured with flesh-piercing spikes, and laid to rest in the dark recesses of a musty tomb. They pass through pain, suffering, death, hell, and—finally—through the passages of time and space into eternal hope.

The gift of transformation is so much more than an engagement ring—a token of God's affection and intentions. It is a sword that not only cuts through flesh and bone, but also severs the cords of sin and decay that bind us to hopelessness. It is truly a two-edged sword: a sword of pain and of redemption. For the Christian, there is no other way.

So where does the Christian's transformational process begin? It *always* begins in hope.

The First Gift of Transformation: Hope

The gift of hope is the first gift of the transformational process, because Christian faith works *from* a basic understanding of who God is, not *toward* one.

At its most basic, the only theology we need to know at the beginning of the transformational journey is this: *Jesus loves me.*

There is an eagerness that usually comes with any important relationship. We anticipate the joy of knowing and being known in such a way that our hearts are filled to the brim with acceptance and love.

There is something refreshingly childlike in how Christ wants us to be in relationship with him.

On one of my bookshelves is a picture of my father walking along a mountain trail with my nephew, Ryan, who was probably two or three years old at the time the picture was taken. Surrounded by pine trees and a small patch of aspen, they walk staring at the ground, a stem of sweet grass jutting from each of their mouths. They are two peas in a pod. They walk heart in heart.

This is exactly where our transformation into the image of God begins. It begins in the heart-knowledge that Christ walks with us. That he matches us stride for stride. That he never will flag in his care and concern for our souls.

We begin in childlike hope because it is children who best understand the kingdom of God. The kingdom is where God is, a child might say. It is where God walks with us.

The Second Gift of Transformation: Truth

I think for many of us the way of transformation is seen as a process of setting an itinerary for the week: a time to get our marching orders established or to fill the spiritual tank with supernatural unleaded. We see it as a time to shine the golden calf to a luster more easily seen.

But consider for a moment an entirely different understanding. In his book *Sabbath,* Wayne Muller says, "In the quiet, the truth emerges: I do not know where I am going. I am riding a wave I cannot see."[1]

Truth's purpose is to reveal what is broken. Its purpose is to break apart our insistence on a smooth-running, secure life.

Just a few days ago a woman wearing a large-billed cap and bright clothes arrived for her scheduled appointment with me. "You look like you're ready to paint the town," I said casually as I motioned for her to take a seat.

"I'm ready to tell the truth," she responded, "and I wore the cap to hide behind and the bright clothes for courage."

Over the years, my sessions with Sonja had been infrequent, at best. I had often encouraged her to be more focused and intentional about the things we were trying to address—her compulsive behaviors, her bouts of depression, her alternating rage and self-loathing.

"I have something to tell you that I should have told you

seven years ago," she continued. "I had an affair with a married man whose wife then killed herself because of the pain and loss it set in motion. The man now lives on the East Coast and his wife is buried in a cemetery I can see from the front window of my home." Her words then ended as abruptly as they had begun.

As she sat weeping, her cap completely covering her face, the only words I could find were, "Thank you for telling me your secret. I think your healing might have finally begun."

At the end of what I can only call a gut-wrenching hour, another appointment was scheduled. I watched her leave through the small garden at the front of my office and up the garden steps. Suddenly, she turned and came back through the front door into my waiting room. I expected a knock at my office door. Had she forgotten something? As I stood to open my office door I heard the waiting room door open and close, and watched as she once again crossed the garden, making her way up the steps and through the garden gate.

Curious, I left my desk and stepped into the waiting room. On a small antique desk near my office door was a large-billed cap. Yes, her healing had begun.

This secret that had held her captive for so many years now, finally could be transformed into a truth that would set her free. Perhaps, I thought as I stepped back into my office and sat in my chair, she could now stop hiding her face in her depression and compulsive behaviors.

Imagine speaking to God the truth about your life. Imagine being so honest with him that you shock yourself. It starts to get a little scary, doesn't it? The thought of being broken, of being exposed in that way, makes the heart race.

I remember the dialogue from the movie *City Slickers,* when Billy Crystal asks his friend what the worst day of his life was. "The day my father left us," his friend says. Caught a little off guard, Crystal then asks, "And what was the best day?" With no hesitation his friend responds, "The same day."

The honesty knocks you over.

Speaking the truth is essential to transformation. To begin changing what is, we need to *say* what is.

The Third Gift of Transformation: Waiting

Three days a week I jog west through my neighborhood of stately trees and old homes, across Colorado Boulevard, to Denver's City Park. If I'm in the park early enough I'll hear the animals in the zoo nearby rousing the world with their cawing and grunting, their chirping and trumpeting.

It was during one of these jogs, as I started making my way around Ferril Lake, that I noticed a man standing just below the entrance to the park's Museum of Nature and Science. He stood by a tripod, obviously preparing to take pictures of the park's spectacular vistas. Looping around the lake, I was surprised to see the man still standing exactly where he had been when I first sighted him.

I finished the jog and went back to my routine, not thinking much about the photographer until two days later when, jogging once again, I saw the same man in the same spot with the same tripod. My curiosity got the best of me.

"I saw you here a couple of days ago," I said in my friendliest tone. "Have you been home since then or have you been standing here for three days?"

"Well," he replied in an equally friendly tone, "I've basically been standing here for three days. I'm waiting."

"Waiting? For what?" I asked.

"I'm not sure," he said, adding, "but I know it'll be worth it when I see it."

Arriving back at the house, I dug around for Robert Bly's translation of, and commentary on, the poems of Rainer Maria Rilke. In particular, I was looking for how Rilke had come to write some of his most famous poems such as "The Panther" and "The Swan." As Bly tells it, the famous sculptor and artist Rodin had one year offered Rilke a job as his secretary. When Rilke confided in Rodin that he hadn't written any poetry in a while, Rodin advised him to go to the zoo. Rilke then inquired of his employer, "What shall I do there?"

"Look at an animal until you see it." replied Rodin. "Two or three weeks might not be too long."[2]

Two or three weeks to look at an animal? You've got to be kidding! And yet, isn't the value of the looking and waiting relative to the value of what we eventually come to see?

What if we knew that, by waiting, we would come to discern God's heart, that we would come to see what he sees? Wouldn't that be worth the wait?

Waiting on God, more than perhaps any other trait of a passionate Christian's life, is the trait that most distinguishes it from modern faith. Waiting gets us out of the way. It removes us from our thrones of productivity and castles of self-sufficiency and places us squarely before the Lion of Judah—watching and waiting to see what we would never be able to see at the pace in which we live. We wait until we no longer realize that we are waiting.

Thomas Merton understood this.

Be still:
There is no longer any need of comment.
It was a lucky wind
That blew away his halo with his cares,
A lucky sea that drowned his reputation.[3]

But—you might say—don't I need at least to stay on top of my actions during this time of waiting so sin won't get in the way? Don't I need to keep my sin detectors on high alert, to keep Satan at bay, so that God can be comfortable being with me?

Well, I suppose, but the order—and, therefore, the emphasis—is wrong.

In regard to sin and its impact on God's life in us, the key thought is this: Sin does not keep God out of my life; it keeps me from seeing that God is, in fact, in my life. Sin does not rob God of his power. It weakens my life because it blinds me to the power of God already in me.

The minute I say that sin hinders God's power, I am saying that his efficacy lies with me. It's up to me whether God is powerful or not.

Rather than first focusing on what I can do about my sin, I should instead be considering who God is and how my only hope is in him. The knowledge that God alone is my sustenance makes me want to dance, cry, and be still, all in one breath. It makes me want to be present, to reach out and grab the powerful, comforting hand of the One who is with me. And, paradoxically, my awareness of his presence leaves less and less room in my life for sin.

In waiting and watching, I trace with my spiritual fingers in the lines of God's face, the cross of Christ. And in this cross I find what I have waited for: intimacy with my God.

The Fourth Gift of Transformation: Sight

The final gift that brings us full circle to the freedom we have in Christ's love is sight.

The twist, however, is that this sight is not what we think of as a restored sight. It is not the kind of sight that gets us back on a trail we've been traveling in the past or a sight that restores our traditional thinking about God and the Christian life. Rather, it is spiritual sight. In the most literal sense I can express, it is a supernatural way of seeing ourselves, our fellow human beings, our path of service and engagement with this world.

This kind of sight sees the higher, narrower trail Greg and I came to enjoy at Mount Holy Cross, as described in chapter 1. This kind of sight sees a human being in the harlot, the gay person, the woman hiding her face behind the bill of her cap, the man in the blue suit, the woman in the blue collar.

This kind of sight sees Christ. It sees the blood and the scars, the joy and the victory, all in one fell swoop. It sees— and embraces—all of life. It sees God.

Instead of calling out, "Lord, come see what I've done for you," it cries out from the depth of its being, "My Lord and my God, I now see what glorious things you have done!"

One Sunday evening our family walked four houses down to a good friend's house for a casual summer cookout. At one point, Anne (our host) said, "Wow, weren't you blown away with that simple, childlike song we sang at church this morning! I was tempted to steal the hymnal so I could copy the words, but my conscience got the better of me."

"Well," I responded, "my conscience told me to grab the hymnal and run. It's been a long time since I've sung a song so dead on the mark with its portrait of spiritual seeing."

Here are the words to the hymn "Not with Naked Eye," written by Daniel Charles Damon. (Yes, I returned the hymnal.)

Not with naked eye, not with human sense:
through the eye of faith observe omnipotence.
God is always near, but is never seen:
Source of heaven and earth and all that lies
between.
Children learn of God trusting what they feel;
touching, tasting, seeking, finding what is real.
Thomas saw the Christ breaking earth's routine;
blessed are those who trust the Holy One unseen.
Not with crafted scope, not with crystal lens:
vision of the Christ begins where seeing ends.[4]

Vision of the Christ begins where seeing ends. Transformation doesn't unfold as greater and greater spiritual attainment. It unfolds as clearer and clearer vision — a vision that is first grounded in childlike hope, broken and purged in the fires of living, soothed and tempered in the balm of waiting, breaking forth at last in a clarity of vision that sees all of life through God's own eyes. Transformation begins where human seeing ends.

The Fruit of Transformation: Love's Freedom

The fruit of transformation is a profound understanding of the utter uselessness of all our manipulative attempts to win God's favor, and a corresponding release into freedom to love and be loved without selfish motive or hidden agenda. Love's freedom is our participation in God's freedom. Jacques Ellul writes: "This is freedom: man's freedom in God's freedom; man's freedom exclusively received in Christ; man's freedom which is free obedience to God and which finds unique expression in childlike acts . . . . "[5]

Those childlike acts include prayer and witness, says Ellul, but also a fundamental attitude toward life that springs from this recognition: "God loved us because he is love and not to get results."[6] On a spiritual level, all our grownup attempts to get results and take control turn into brackish water. Speaking through the prophet Jeremiah,

God said: "My people have committed two sins: They have forsaken me, the spring of living water, and have dug their own cisterns, broken cisterns that cannot hold water."[7]

Those who return to Jesus Christ daily with childlike faith and without any intent other than to be completely his and to live in his will discover that "as the Scripture has said, streams of living water will flow from within him."[8]

chapter 9

HOW RELATIONSHIPS
ARE TRANSFORMED

They were poor, as country people have
often been, but they had each other;
they had each other's comfort when
they needed it, and they had their stories,
their history together in that place.
WENDELL BERRY, *What Are People For?*

———————— ≈ ————————

aige and I have a game we play. At bedtime,
after I have gotten her started with pajamas
and other rituals of the night, we call down to Beth: "Time
for prayers and songs!" As Beth starts up the stairs toward
Paige's room, Paige cries out, "We're not in here!" and then
ducks under the covers, or in the closet, or in some other
dark place to hide.

Heeding an urgent, "Daddy, over here!" I quickly join
her in the darkness to await the sound of Beth's feet

padding down the hall and into the room.

In that brief half-minute, there is little conversation. Excitedly squeezing my arm or neck, Paige sometimes whispers to me, "Daddy, don't be afraid." By then, our heads are pressed so tightly together that when Beth enters the room, we leap from the darkness as one. We are suddenly Four-Eyed Monster scaring the beejeepers out of Beth (who, of course, graciously indulges the charade, time and time again).

The passionate person sees in a story like this the delight of companionship—the gift of fellowship in the heart of the adventure. She is passionate about the knowledge that even in darkness there is fellowship and hope, regardless of how it might sometimes seem.

An old Hasidic tale goes like this:

An old Rabbi once asked his pupils how they could tell when the night had ended and the day had begun.

"Could it be," asked one of the students, "when you can see an animal in the distance and tell whether it's a sheep or a dog?"

"No," answered the Rabbi.

Another asked, "Is it when you can look at a tree in the distance and tell whether it's a fig tree or a peach tree?"

"No," answered the Rabbi.

"Then what is it?" the pupils demanded.

"It is when you can look on the face of any man or woman and see that it is your sister or brother. Because if you cannot see this, it is still night."[1]

I don't suggest that all religions lead to the same place or that we should just all hold hands and become one with the universe. But I do suggest that we dispense with the idea that there is an elite core of Christians who have figured out God's especially blessed ways. "No temptation has seized you except what is common to man," wrote the apostle Paul (1 Corinthians 10:13). While we're on this earth, we have an indelible, common bond in our broken humanity, which should lead us to be welcoming, large-hearted, and gentle with one another.

We each suffer, enjoy, grieve, and touch with the same human body as everyone else. And the only difference I see between the passionate Christian's life and anyone else's—and granted, it is a huge one—is that keeping aware of Christ in the middle of whatever is going on in life fills the passionate one with a sense that there is reason not only to hope, but also to celebrate. But instead of making us cocky, this awareness humbles us. We are grateful that lives such as ours can make any sense at all, and we want not only to share this hope with others, but to share *in it* with them as well.

There is such freedom in letting go of our jostling for position. We are forever evaluating others competitively, sizing them up, keeping our distance from them, holding ourselves in check. The freedom of transformation—the freedom of love—is opening ourselves up to people as those who struggle in this life just as we do.

Placing myself in the mindset to see and clasp the hand of God and the hands of my companions in the midst of this present life immerses me in the passionate, imaginative fellowship of faith.

THE NIGHT THE POWER WENT OUT, AND WHAT HAPPENED THEN

I can't remember the exact occasion. Was it Thanksgiving, or Christmas? Perhaps it was New Year's. I would guess that I was ten or twelve years old.

The first snapshot of this event is a scene of between thirty and forty men, women, and children—aunts, uncles, and cousins of every size and shape—excitedly jostling about in the living room of my grandparents' single-story farmhouse.

Abandoning any hope of escape, we had all opted to sit tight and wait out the heavy, crippling snowstorm that had caught us off guard.

Multiplying like Jesus' loaves of bread and fishes, enough bedding and pillows to hold us through the night seemed as if by magic to appear from car trunks, from tractor cabins, and from the house's small bedrooms, closets, and chests.

Because the three back bedrooms were notoriously cold—storm or not—it made sense for the parents to brave out the night in these rooms while the kids cozied-up near the wood-burning stove in the living room.

At some point in the evening's settling-in, the power flickered, and the lights went out. I remember how relatively unconcerned the adults were by this loss of power. Having shared the majority of their lives together on this farm, they had undoubtedly been faced with far more challenging events than this one. No power? No problem.

Glowing through the small, mica-paned windows of the stove, a warm and robust firelight caught the edges of our sleeping bags and blankets, casting a spell over the room. I remember it distinctly: I lay facing to the north with my head propped on a ridge in the floor that ran the full east-west distance of the room. The stove, to my right, was about five feet away. I was delirious with joy.

What wonderful turn of fate was this that I would be surrounded by these people, this warmth, this assurance that our little house in a sea of snow would keep itself aright through the ebbs and swells of this dark night?

The giggles and voices were finally beginning to taper when, suddenly, the back door blew open and the sound of a man's heavy boots and labored breathing entered the house. From my vantage point on the floor, I could see, making its way through the kitchen and then toward the living room, a large, hunch-backed form.

I held my breath.

"Hey, Buck!" it said. "Help me out here."

One of my uncles, already making his way through the maze of children, responded, "Here, Dad, . . . hand her to me."

My grandfather lifted a newborn calf—the silhouetted "hunch" I'd seen—from his shoulders and handed it to my uncle. "We'll need a little room by the fire here," he whispered.

Again I was surprised by how little was said.

With some minor adjustments and compacting of bodies, a place was cleared and a blanket laid by the fire for our new guest. Within minutes the calf stopped shivering and seemed quite content with his new digs.

The room was rich in earthy textures. The smell of wet

calf, the squeaking wood floor, the lingering coolness from a briefly opened door, the body heat of twenty or so children stacked together like herringboned bricks, the firelight, the iced-over windows.

In the midst of calamities both real and imagined, in the heart of a dark, cold night, our lives were bound to each other by more than blood. By hand and by heart we were keeping each other warm, sacrificing for each other, welcoming the cold and frightened into our company. We had no light, no immediate path of escape, and barely enough heat.

But we had everything. We were liberated from all but the need to be a family and to take care of one another. With the calf, we had been born that night into love's freedom.

THE TRANSFORMATIONAL JOURNEY

Now there is an inherent danger in what I've said to this point. The danger is that we might begin to get the picture that our relationships with each other are to be cozy and secure, the warm glow of firelight dancing on our hair, the bucolic calf lying snugly at our feet. Unless we're careful, we might fall into the common trap of thinking that the point of our fellowship is to help each other figure out what needs fixing so we can all, in Amish fashion, raise each other's barns and keep each other's children in line.

Certainly, our fellowship of faith involves such things. But this fixing and mending is never to be the reason for our fellowship. We are bound together by two things: our absolute depravity and brokenness, and our awareness that there is no hope for intimacy with God—or with each other—aside from the reconciling work of Christ on the cross.

And as much as we might wish it otherwise, the transformational template doesn't change when we shift from the self to the community at large. As self is transformed by Christ, so too are our relationships.

How Relationships Are Transformed

In the previous chapter, I described a pattern of transformation, four phases that can help us be aware and sensitive to what God may be doing in each of our lives. We can see this pattern repeatedly in the Bible. I believe it is a guide for revitalizing our relationships.

On the transformational journey, we are first given a vision, perhaps even an experience, of hope and certainty. This was the *hope* Jesus inspired in the disciples during the early days of his ministry—the grand hope of the kingdom of God, the kingdom of love's freedom, a completely new way of relating to one another.

Second, transformation moves to expose the difficult

truths in our lives. We see this in the lives of the disciples—James and John jostling for privileged places in the kingdom, Peter's dark and agonizing recognition that he had failed his Lord and his high commitment to "go with you to prison and to death" (Luke 22:33).

Third, in our brokenness, we find ourselves *waiting* on God and his ways. In spite of their despair at the start of their journey on the Emmaus road, the two disciples waited on the stranger in puzzlement as they walked with him, searching his face for answers, transfixed by his unfolding of the meaning of Israel's history.

And finally, we are given new *sight*. Our eyes of flesh become eyes of spirit. When Jesus broke the bread at the Emmaus inn, the disciples recognized him, and he vanished. He vanished from their eyes of flesh—but not from their eyes of spirit. There he blazed in their minds.

Hope, truth, waiting, sight.

Relationships in transformation (relationships of any sort—romantic, familial, the Christian community, friendships) will follow this same course.

One thing that books about relationships never get right is the second stage of transformation: the importance of having the whole thing fall apart or, in transformational terms, of seeing the truth. Whether friendship, courtship, marriage, or fellowship, a relationship based on the joys of basking in each other's presence is a relationship standing on one incredibly anemic foot. Until a thing falls, it thinks it rules the universe.

In his book *Learning to Fall,* Philip Simmons—well into the debilitating stages of ALS (Lou Gehrig's disease)—reflects on his humbling fall down a flight of stairs: "In the Christian theology of the fall, we all suffer the fall from grace, the fall from our primordial connectedness with God. My little tumble down the stairs was my own expulsion from the Garden: ever after I have been falling forward and down into the scarred years of conscious life, falling into the knowledge of pain, grief, and loss."[2]

The falls we take in our relationships move us forward and down as well. Instead of a physical death, however, the death we experience is the death of the false idol of idealism about relationships. Dietrich Bonhoeffer wrote:

Just as surely as God desires to lead us to a knowledge of genuine Christian fellowship, so surely must we be overwhelmed by a great disillusionment with others, with Christians in general, and, if we are fortunate, with ourselves. Only that fellowship which faces such disillusionment, with all its unhappy and ugly aspects, begins to be what it should be in God's sight, begins to grasp in faith the promise that is given.[3]

False notions of what relationships are required to do for us must eventually take the fall down the stairs. They must, so to speak, fall head over heels into truth.

In response to my question to married couples, "So why did you two marry, anyway?" I have yet to hear the answer, "To be transformed, of course." No, we marry to settle down, to tie the knot, to grow old together. To be transformed? Whatever does that have to do with relationships?

But relationships are the contexts of our transformation. "As iron sharpens iron, so one man sharpens another."[4] Relationships are where the impact and efficacy of the Cross is most visibly seen.

At a friend's fiftieth birthday celebration, the "guys"— being the guys we are—eventually made our way to the hosts' back porch to toast our friend's new old-guy status with some really nasty cigars. In the course of our male bonding, stories of relationships began bubbling to the surface. "We're on our third therapist," said one celebrant. "I still don't know if we're going to make it. We're just really different."

"I'd be tempted to bag it," said the guy next to him. "Don't you sometimes wonder if it's really worth it?"

This brief interchange is a microcosm of the question we all ask, if only to ourselves: Are relationships worth it? Is my relationship to my husband, my family of origin—yes, even my faith—worth the suffering I go through to try to make it work?

Even when the answer is yes, the reasons I hear seem to fall along the lines of "yes, because that's how we grow," "yes, because it's the Christian thing to do," "yes, because it's the commitment that's important." But is there another reason to stick with our commitments that trumps personal growth, Christian responsibility, and commitment for commitment's sake? I think there is. My "yes" would be, "yes, because that's where God is."

What? Is that it?

Well, yes. I asked in chapter 4, If God isn't there in our pain and suffering, then where is he? When we stop expecting our relationships to be our saving, golden calf, we can begin to see God's presence in our relationships' challenges.

This doesn't mean that serious issues will no longer need to be addressed or that the party on the other end of the relationship will see the matter the same way. What it does mean is that the emphasis on "making it work" will take a back seat to "seeing God in it."

As we will now see, this dynamic also plays out in similar fashion in our approach to fellowship as a whole.

How Fellowship Is Transformed

For me, the initial promise of faith was that I would inherit the peace, the power, and the protection of God. Peace, power, and protection: what could be better?

My own disillusionment (my fall into truth) came in waves: The first wave was the realization that there were some pretty broken people in the Christian community. One man I had considered a mentor committed suicide. Another was exposed as having had as many as twenty affairs over the twelve years of his marriage. A woman who had led many women to Christ fell into a depression from which—as far as I know—she has never emerged. Like ghouls rising from their midnight graves, the wounded, broken, and dead began walking through the walls of my pretenses and well-secured theology. Any attempt to hold them at bay seemed to spawn a multiplicative phenomenon. Ghouls everywhere.

The second wave hit when I realized my quiver of newly acquired spiritual gifts were inadequate to deeply change the unbecoming characters invading my spiritual party. Tongues, baptisms, Scripture memorization, moving from fellowship to fellowship—none of it helpful. The ghouls kept coming.

The third wave hit when I had a dream. It was one of those dreams—what therapists call a lucid dream—in which you are aware that you are dreaming and so you go along for the ride, knowing you can change things in the dream at will, if you'd like.

In this dream, I was riding belly down on something

akin to a glider, floating along through a large meadow—
one I could identify in real life as a meadow in the foothills
just west of Fort Collins, Colorado.

In a way that happens only in dreams, out of the
meadow began rising the bodies of people I knew in real
life—some dead and some still living. The strange thing
was that I recognized them by their backs. There was
Grandma Brown's slightly bent-over form with a shawl
across her back; there was the balding head of the man who
took his own life; the strikingly beautiful hair of an old girl-
friend; the muscular torso of my high school gymnastics
coach. The bodies kept rising.

This is my dream, I thought—suppose I rev up my
glider and swoop down on them from the front.

As I came around the field, turning into the faces of the
people rising from the ground, something happened in the
dream that I couldn't control: all of their faces became mine.
Everything else in the dream instantly disappeared: the
glider, the meadow, the sense of space and time. All I could
see were dozens of bodies—with my face on the head of
each one of them.

I woke with a start—and instantly fell headlong into my
own truth: I am not only one of the wounded; I am all of
them. I saw in an instant my complete solidarity with all
those figures before me.

To me, this was not a dream about the universality of our common humanity. It was a dream about our common brokenness and need for Christ. Strangely, this truth has become the pivotal source of a new joy in my Christian life that has remained with me since the dream. It was the breaking of one more fetter that was keeping me from love's freedom.

My friends, and especially my wife, often ask me how I can have such an instant rapport with the hand-to-mouth artists, the street people, the pierced, the heavily tattooed, and the scruffy throwaways hanging out in Denver's LoDo district. I suppose the expected thing to say would be that, knowing I have something to offer them that they don't have, I love them with the love of Christ.

But that's not what I would say.

I would say it's not that I have something they don't have, but rather that I am what they are. I am just as broken, just as lost, just as resistant to transformation. But, by God's grace, I know someone who knows the way through the mess. I know someone who is the way.

And so it is with the community of faith. Fellowship committed to transformation is a fellowship of many bodies with one face. But whose face is it? Yours? Mine?

It is the face of One who has established by his incarnation the most profound solidarity with each of us—the one who is intent on shaping us into his holy dwelling. It is the face of Christ.

And the rag-tag fellowship that wears his face also walks with his feet and heals with his hands. It is a fellowship of the broken—but a fellowship that is beginning to see as God sees.

chapter 10

HOW SERVICE IS TRANSFORMED

A fable: once upon a time, there was a crown so
heavy that it could only be worn by one who
remained completely oblivious to its glitter.
DAG HAMMARSKJOLD, *Markings*

Almost anyone can feed the poor.

Almost anyone can help the elderly, be an
AIDS worker in Africa, help the illiterate learn to read,
take in an orphan. One's service to his fellow human
being can be—and is daily—administered by people of
every race, religion, philosophical bent, and sexual orientation. And wouldn't it be tidy for the Christian if these
efforts were ineffectual? Wouldn't it be kudos for us if
every effort to help by those who don't follow Christ came
to naught? The reason it didn't work, we could say, is

because the effort didn't have Christ in it.

But it does work—and often much better than a Christian's effort to provide the same service.

So what is different about Christian service? How is the Christian's efforts to impact her community and her world any different from anyone else's? And what does Christian service have to do with transformation?

THE SERVANT'S SOURCE

When we think of the word *service,* many common activities come to mind: being served at a restaurant, a tennis service, enlisting in the service, serving one's country, serving God.

The motion seems always to be outward. I come with tools, or expectations, or advantage of perspective that I then give, or extend, or share with someone else. The image is accurate: service will always have that kind of effect—it will attempt to meet a need, often in very direct fashion.

But, again, we have to consider how Christian service is different. If it is not different in its capacity to identify and meet needs, then what is the difference? For the answer, let's go back to how transformation works.

I have suggested that transformation's third stage is *waiting.* Looking at the swan, the panther, God's face, until we see it.

I think this waiting stage is the majority of our existence. I think it is spiritually designed this way because it is in the waiting stage, more than any other, that we are most dependent, most acutely aware, most present with God.

And I think that the majority of our truly spiritual service occurs in this stage—in the stage of waiting on God.

This waiting is critical to the Christian's service because it keeps her flexible and alert; it keeps her available for the surprises that come with knowing God. It keeps us from saying, "Here's what I will do for God," and shifts the focus to "By God's grace, here's what I will be." I will be available. I will rest in God and follow wherever he takes me.

True Christian service is never about the service, as service; it is about seeing and bringing to light the presence of God in the midst of whatever need we seek to attend. However gallant and exceptional, the effort may or may not be effective. Ultimately, the efficacy of the effort is subordinate to the revelation of God's presence in the effort—*and that we can't control.* And yet we still give our very best to our service because it is in our being God's that he is able to give himself to others in whatever ways he may choose.

In the days of his flesh, even Christ's service, as service, had its limitations. Lazarus still died eventually. (At least, I assume he did—I haven't seen him around lately.) The lady at the well undoubtedly went back to sinning—at least in some form. Champions of faith endured their own calamities and ailments: Paul had his eyes; Timothy had his stomach. The fixing and the curing may be the context of our service, but it is not the reason for it. The effort might be effective. And it might not. Ultimately, the efficacy of the effort is not what matters most.

We serve in some particular way because we are waiting on God and that's where he has us. We bring our hands, our love, and our passion for God's presence to our effort and—in that same passionate spirit—we give ourselves away to those for whom God's Son gave his life.

The difference between service and Christian service is the servant's source.

The Christian's reason for being—and thus for serving—is God and God alone. Who am I to say how God will or should use my efforts? If my life is not about God, then it will be about myself, it will be about how effective I can be "for God's kingdom."

Thus I do *all* that I do as unto God, which means waiting on him as the source—the strength and will—of my service.

The Servant's Heart

It is unfortunate that the term "a servant's heart" seems immediately to evoke the image of a geisha girl—head bowed, moving stealthily about her immaculate realm— dutifully attending to the needs of her master. It is a fragile, demur image that stands at odds with what I think of as a servant.

Instead I see muscularity. I see C. S. Lewis's stamping horse. I see Rilke's swan *and* his panther. I see on the body and in the countenance of God's servant the scars and calluses and sun-leathered face of one who has truly, intentionally engaged his life. I see a servant so immersed in God that not even death itself can stand in her way.

Dag Hammarskjold says it this way:

Tomorrow we shall meet,
Death and I—
And he shall thrust his sword
Into one who is wide awake.[1]

That's what I see: one who is wide awake. Paying attention. Heart and soul panting for a chance, if God should call, to pull the wagon, climb the mountain.

The heart of a servant is by nature torn in two. It wants

to do and it wants to be. It wants to rest—it really does—but it races, nevertheless.

For the passionate, imaginative Christian, this is what it comes to: waiting in faith, hope, and love. Straining to see how God's kingdom will next show itself on this earth. Longing to know how its spark of transformation might begin to glow and radiate in the darkest places of the world. Longing to see one more imprisoned heart liberated by love's freedom.

The tug we feel is a tug like that of a calf being born, the horse's tug on the bit before the gate opens. It is the tug of one who waits, coming finally into a glimmer of what life looks like through God's eyes.

From the annals of "What was I thinking?" comes this embarrassing account of a *doulos* (Greek for *servant*) trip about twenty years ago to several struggling churches near Bozeman, Montana.

Being one of the adult leaders of my church's high school ministry, it was my job to make sure I got our kids back home to Colorado in one piece, which I was able to accomplish with great flourish, I might add. Getting *myself* back, however, was another story.

Somewhere on the route back from Bozeman to Colorado Springs is a canyon—a deep one; one of those canyons where you feel compelled to let the mesmerizing swoon of standing on its rim pull you over and into its gaping mouth—perhaps a thousand feet straight down.

At any rate, there I stood, hands on the hefty, black iron railing, leaning out and over to get a glimpse of where the canyon took an abrupt turn to the south.

The awe and anticipation were causing my heart to race; just one more stretch of the neck and I would see the canyon's majestic . . . and over I went! My sandals flew through the air as I made a fruitless attempt to save myself. Over the railing I went and—thank God—onto a small rock ledge about three or four feet directly below. Needless to say, I quickly scrambled back to the railing, my knees bleeding and my head swimming, to the ashen faces of those who had watched me go over.

The heart of a Christian servant is forever on this earth leaning, looking, stretching itself to its limits to catch a glimpse of God's majesty. We chomp at the bit, and then we reel in frustration and perhaps exhaustion, in our attempts to see God at work. Our hearts pound in anticipation, only to be partly satisfied. Yes, he is here, right now, I see him . . . *and* I see that there is still so much more about him to see. Yes, my service to God is effective . . . *and* then it appears that it's not.

The tug is relentless. It is the tug of seeing through a glass only darkly but, nevertheless, seeing.

Whatever joy the servant's heart knows, then, cannot be dependent on what it sees with the naked eye. If it is looking for hope in miraculous healings or potent solutions to pain and suffering, it will only partly—if at all—be satisfied. If it is looking for a system of faith that will solve the dilemmas of parenting, courtship, or career, the system will most certainly break down.

The servant's heart is a heart abandoned to God, and nothing else. And the servant's essential joy is the joy of being with God. Out of this servant's heart will flow the love and will of God, because his heart is God's heart. From this servant's hands will flow God's strength, and with the soles of her feet she will walk the truer way.

THE SERVANT'S LEGACY

A Legacy of Truth and Love

For the longest time I wondered how it was even possible that the apostle Paul could say of himself in 2 Timothy 4:7, "I have fought the good fight, I have finished the race, I have kept the faith." Hadn't he earlier in his life referred to himself as the "chief of sinners"? Hadn't he said that he couldn't understand why he did the things he didn't want to do and didn't do the things he wanted to do?

So how could he claim any spiritual victory whatsoever,

given his perpetually sinful condition? I think it was because he finally came to see that his sinful condition was not his identity.

His sin could prod him, poke him, puff itself up, disguise itself as an angel of light and fan into flames the embers of Paul's pride. It could knock him down, but it could never knock him out.

Sin wanted to be everything in Paul's life. It wanted to make Paul so sin-conscious that he could think of nothing else. But Paul wouldn't have it. He finished the race, not as a perfect person, but as one who had found himself in Christ. He could say that he had kept the faith because he had stayed close to God. He could finally be content— whatever the circumstances—because he had come to see life through God's eyes.

The legacy the passionate Christian leaves has virtually nothing to do with getting sin under control or managing the pain of living. It has everything to do with learning to *love*. And love has everything to do with knowing the kind of truth about yourself and others that sets you free.

When I think of my grandfather Clifford Allen, the fiddler, I think of one who was set free, one who was so comfortable in his skin that he could love with a joyful, unself-conscious, large-hearted love. His attitude toward life was one of celebration, of freely reveling in the presence of

God and other people, even though he knew so well the harsh realities of farm life in eastern Colorado.

I think this was the apostle Paul's secret too. Paul could say that he had run the race because he was free. Not free from his sinning, just free from the weight of it. Imperfect, yes, but nevertheless whole. Free to see that his true identity was rock-solid in Christ.

A Legacy of Intimacy with God

The most intimate moments of my life have almost always taken me by surprise.

There was the first Thanksgiving visit back home on college break when I entered the kitchen—duffle bag still in hand—and was greeted not by my father's handshake, but by his open arms. There was the time I had shared, for the first time in my life, a deep, intimate pain with a good friend and looked up through the misery of my tears to see him tearful as well.

And then there was the time, after an especially long and difficult day, that I lay exhausted on my seven-month-old daughter's bedroom floor as she played and babbled to herself several feet away. Eyes closed, I suddenly felt small, gentle fingers, toes, and knees working their way across my stomach and onto my chest. With a coo and a sigh, my daughter fell fast asleep on my pounding, overwhelmingly grateful heart.

What strikes me in these examples is their spontaneity, their lack of manipulation, their absence of staging. Instead there is a waiting love—an expectant waiting on the surprises of God in the course of everyday existence.

It is not so much the staging that dictates our level of intimacy with God as it is the spontaneous nature of a love relationship, in which all staging falls away. Yes, there is intention. There is watching, hope, and expectancy. There is a conscious making room in our hearts for God. But there is freedom from the programmatic and the overly calculated.

For the modern Christian—with the power of technology to create visual wonders with surround sound—there is a great temptation to see spiritual staging as a precursor to intimacy with God. In other words, there is the trap of thinking that an intimate relationship with God requires an event-inducing atmosphere—something big and memorable.

But the legacy of intimacy with God that a passionate servant leaves is, surprisingly, a comparatively uneventful one—so quiet it is almost subversive. It is uneventful because the intimacy is the norm, not the exception.

Just imagine it: a relationship with God where the intimacy is the norm, not the exception.

I think this means that we need to look much more closely at the people in our lives, the struggles in our hearts, and the stones lining our desert paths. I think it means what

I've been suggesting from the beginning of this book: that we look for God in the more commonplace life, that we learn to see him with a different set of eyes.

The legacy I hope to leave my family, friends, and community of faith is a legacy that attests to the relentlessly intimate nature of God's presence in my life.

Please, God, let me look for you not in burning bushes or flights of angels. Let me see you instead in my brother's face and my sister's pain. Let me see you skipping with the children, laughing with the bus driver, listening intently to the woman in the coffee shop who lost her child six months ago. Let me wait, and live, in the intimacy of your love, and then let me pass the legacy on.

A Legacy of Passionate, Imaginative Faith

The Christian is grounded in a hope so ancient and yet so fresh. This hope flows freely through time and space. It is the hope of purpose and meaning, the hope that this life will make some kind of sense and that it is redeemed in Christ for some special purpose.

Although the story is at one level complex and even mysterious, the essence of it is straightforward: humankind's relationship with God has been broken. In the cross of Christ we have God's sacrificial reparation. And this reparation unfolds to transform the person who—

recognizing with awe the height and depth of God's love—trusts Christ to go before him as he engages his faith with his world.

The intimacy of this journey with God is what I have been calling the passionate, imaginative faith. It is a faith that takes risks, a faith that often steps into the unknown with no other confidence than the conviction that the God who provided water in the desert yesterday is utterly dependable for tomorrow's needs as well. It is a faith that resonates with Paul's words: "And my God will meet all your needs according to his glorious riches in Christ Jesus" (Philippians 4:19).

This risk of the passionate one is not always a risk of doing. Waiting is often a risk. So is telling the truth. So is daring to imagine what God sees, instead of insisting on the security of seeing a thing—a marriage, a faith, a child, a way of reconciliation—in a tidy, packaged form.

I believe the greatest risks we will take in our spiritual lives are the ones that unfold directly in front of us. It is risky to imagine that something refreshing and sustaining really *can* and *does* flow from stone.

But this is what the passionate faith strives to imagine. The abundance it sees is not an abundance of quantity or quality—it is an abundance of redeemed sight. An abundance of seeing life the way God sees it.

In the opening story in chapter 1 of Greg and me at Mount Holy Cross, we came to see—with the fisherman's guidance—another trail. What, a trail . . . up there? Yes, another way—right there in front of our faces. And the architect we hired to design our home's addition saw in our painting a stunning beauty—not just in the deft strokes and vibrant colors of the picture itself, but also in the complementary grace of its damaged frame.

In my opening invitation to this book, I told the story of the horse and buggy and the powerful eighteen wheeler that exhibits pragmatism's attempt to cram Right Christian Living into our lives. But in the end that approach inspires us to nothing, except to get out of its way as quickly as possible.

Unless we can see that even in the midst of circumstances that may or may not change, God *still* makes a difference—in our character, in our trust in his dependability, in our love for family, friends, and strangers—we will be sucked into the eighteen wheeler's roaring airstream. We will get caught up in a pursuit of the visible, the successful—and our hearts will grow numb again.

The passionate way is for the one whose life has come—perhaps many times—to a crossroad, to a place where she is finally willing to consider another way of seeing, another possibility.

No, not the possibility of another life or another God, but the possibility that within this given life—and within the intimate arms of this God who redeems us in ways that are beyond all we hope or imagine—is the abundance of living we so longingly seek . . . water from stone.

DISCUSSION SESSIONS

---~---

*P*erhaps this book has been prompting questions or changes in perspective that you may
want to discuss with a friend or a group you participate in.
For further thought, here are some possible discussion-
starters you may want to explore. The sessions proposed
below don't necessarily follow the chapter outline. In fact,
you may want to explore these questions after reading the
entire book.

a. In the book's opening "Invitation to a Journey," the
metaphor used to describe today's Christian faith is that
of an eighteen wheeler "spitting ice and spraying steam
and slush from its wheels and iron nostrils." Do you think
this metaphor fairly portrays the general tone of our
modern faith? Reflecting on your own experience of
Christian worship, ministry, and faith journey, is the

image too strong, not strong enough, or completely off the mark?

b. Part 1 suggests that industriousness, numbness (which easily morphs into cynicism), and passion represent three basic frames of mind of today's Christian faith. Is your own orientation to faith one of these three, or would you add a fourth? Or, if your faith looks like a hybrid of these three, what percentage on a pie chart would you allocate to each one?

c. The title of this book, *Water from Stone*, suggests that it is from the very common and very apparent "stones" lining our lives' paths that God's refreshing and immediate presence flows forth. For you personally, is this a difficult concept to buy into? In your most honest personal assessment, are you one who seeks God in this way, or do you tend toward a more dramatic, golden god "who will go before you" (Exodus 32:1)?

d. In part 2 the author chose to discuss certainty, mystery, fragmentation, and wholeness as four concepts of faith that—if we are to see God's transformational ways more clearly—need revisiting. Why do you think he chose these four? What do you think of his statement in chapter 7 that "whatever wholeness we find on this earth . . . will be seasoned with a sadness that is nevertheless blessed and without bitterness," and that "rather than being an achieved perfection, this kind of wholeness is more a redeemed imperfection"?

e. The author suggests in part 3 that the path of transformation involves, in general, four stages: hope, (a fall into) truth, waiting, and sight. Which stage(s) do we as a community of faith (and perhaps you, in particular) most often emphasize? What is it about the other stages that make them less appealing?

f. If applied to the community of faith at large, how do you think the following three perspectives might change the nature of our worship, fellowship, and service: (1) the awareness that God is with us here, now . . . regardless of how it might sometimes seem; (2) that God derives his deepest pleasure not so much from our industriousness as from our transformation into "love's freedom," which is the conditionless mutuality of love God wants to share with us; and (3) that our transformation occurs *within* the relationships and commitments we've already made, however challenging?

g. Which idea(s) in this book, if taken seriously, do you think would most transform your own journey of faith?

NOTES

INVITATION TO A JOURNEY

1. Eugene H. Peterson, "To the Suburban Church of North America," *Christianity Today*, October 25, 1999, p. 67.

2. Exodus 3:8.

3. Psalm 18:19.

4. Anthony Giddens, *The Consequences of Modernity* (Stanford, CA: Stanford University Press), 1990, p. 114.

5. Psalm 78:19-20.

6. William Barrett, *The Illusion of Technique* (Garden City, NJ: Anchor Books), 1978, p. 322.

chapter 1: IMAGINING A TRUER WAY

1. Fourteeners are Colorado's mountains that rise 14,000 feet or more above sea level.

2. Jacques Ellul, trans. Geoffrey W. Bromiley, *The Politics of God and the Politics of Man* (Grand Rapids, MI: William B. Eerdmans Publishing Company), 1972, p. 192.

3. Luke 24:29.

4. Dallas Willard, "The Key to the Keys of the Kingdom," a previously unpublished paper on the website www.dwillard.com.

chapter 2: IMAGINING A REFRESHING GOD

1. Edward Hirsch, *How to Read a Poem* (New York: Harcourt Brace, 1999), p. 27.

2. C. S. Lewis, *The Great Divorce* (New York: Macmillan, 1946), p. 102.

3. Anne Lamott, quoted in Agnieszka Tennant, "'Jesusy' Anne Lamott," *Christianity Today,* January 2003, p. 56.

chapter 3: IMAGINING THE PRESENT

1. Annie Dillard, *Pilgrim at Tinker Creek* (New York: HarperPerennial, 1999), p. 81.

chapter 5: SEEING MYSTERY

1. Hebrews 11:8.

2. Walter Brueggemann, *The Prophetic Imagination* (Minneapolis: Fortress Press, 2001), p. 1.

chapter 6: SEEING FRAGMENTATION

1. Wendell Berry, *Life Is a Miracle* (Washington, D.C.: Counterpoint, 2000), p. 103.

2. Lyrics from the hymn "A Mighty Fortress Is Our God."

3. Isaiah 57:15b.

4. *A Wish For Wings That Work*, Berkeley Breathed, prod. Peggy Regan, dir. Skip Jones, 30 min., Universal Cartoon Studio, 1991, videocassette.

chapter 7: SEEING WHOLENESS

1. J. R. R. Tolkien, *The Lord of The Rings: The Return of the King* (Boston: Houghton Mifflin, 1991), p. 1067, (emphasis added).

2. Søren Kierkegaard, *Fear and Trembling,* trans. W. Lowrie, (1941; reprint, New York: Doubleday, 1954), p. 45.

chapter 8: HOW SELF IS TRANSFORMED

1. Wayne Muller, *Sabbath* (New York: Bantam Books, 1999), p. 189.

2. Robert Bly, trans., *Selected Poems of Rainer Maria Rilke* (New York: Harper and Row, 1981), p. 133.

3. Patrick Hart and Jonathan Montaldo, eds., *The Intimate Merton* (New York: HarperSanFrancisco, 1999), p. 269.

4. Daniel Charles Damon, from the hymnal *Worship & Rejoice* (Carol Stream, Ill.: Hope, 2001), p. 417.

5. Jacques Ellul, *The Politics of God and the Politics of Man* (Grand Rapids, MI: William B. Eerdmans Publishing Company), 1972, p. 199.

6. Ellul, p. 197.

7. Jeremiah 2:13.

8. John 7:38, (NIV assumed).

chapter 9: HOW RELATIONSHIPS ARE TRANSFORMED

1. Frederic and Mary Ann Brussat, eds., *Spiritual Literacy* (New York: Scribner, 1996), p. 502.

2. Philip Simmons, *Learning to Fall* (New York: Bantam, 2002), p. 3.

3. Dietrich Bonhoeffer, *Life Together,* trans. John Doberstein (New York: Harper and Row, 1954), pp. 26-27.

4. Proverbs 27:17.

chapter 10: HOW SERVICE IS TRANSFORMED

1. Dag Hammarskjold, *Markings,* trans. Leif Sjoberg and W. H. Auden (New York: Knopf, 1964), p. 6.

Author

---~---

WAYNE BROWN is a therapist, speaker, and author. He has advanced degrees in both counseling (LMFT) and theology (M.Div. from Fuller Seminary). His first book, *Living the Renewed Life*, won The 2000 Colorado Book Award. A member of the American Association of Marriage and Family Therapists and the American Counseling Association, Wayne specializes in counseling those in the high-profile worlds of media and professional athletics. His wife, Beth, is a federal bankruptcy judge. They live in Denver with their five-year-old daughter, Paige.

FAITH ISN'T A TO-DO LIST, IT'S A RELATIONSHIP.

The Rabbi's Heartbeat

In this powerful book, best-selling author Brennan Manning challenges readers of all ages to become real with Christ and live their lives without hiding or posing as perfect.

by Brennan Manning
1-57683-469-7

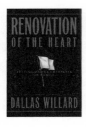

Renovation of the Heart

You can shed sinful habits and increasingly take on the character of Christ through "the transformation of the spirit," a personal apprenticeship with Jesus Christ.

by Dallas Willard
1-57683-296-1

Inside Out

If you want a more vital union with God and a deeper sense of personal wholeness, let this book help you discover how God works real, liberating change when you live from the inside out.

by Larry Crabb
1-57683-082-9